# WHOM ALONE WE WORSHIP AND SERVE

What the Bible teaches
about God

BY

ROBERT P. MILLS

PLC PUBLICATIONS
1998

# Whom Alone We Worship and Serve
## What the Bible Teaches about God

© 1998 PLC Publications

PO Box 2210
Lenoir, NC 28645

Cover art by Kristin Searfoss
Cover design and printing by **Print**Systems, Inc.

First printing

ISBN 0-9652602-1-6

Library of Congress Catalog Card Number 98-91306

Printed in the United States of America

# Contents

# Introduction

The only really important question before us today is this:
"What do you mean by God?"
*Alfred North Whitehead*

The title of this study, *Whom Alone We Worship and Serve*, is taken from "A Brief Statement of Faith."[1] It serves as a constant reminder that the subject of these lessons is not an impersonal abstraction, but the Triune God, a living person to whom we properly respond with worship, service, and love. The goal of this study is to help participants grow in their knowledge of what Scripture and the Church have said about God, and thereby to grow in their knowledge of God.

## How are these studies organized?

Each lesson begins with a brief overview and the reading of one or two biblical texts. The studies are then divided into three sections: The Text, The Teachings, and The Life of the Church. Discussion questions conclude each of these sections.

The Text *identifies* key words and phrases in the biblical text and explores them in some detail. Taking the time to read and consider the other Scripture references given in this section will yield valuable insights into the verses being studied. Unless otherwise indicated, Scripture quotations are taken from the New International Version.

The Teachings *explain* the historic Christian doctrines that have emerged from these biblical texts. Christians need to study Scripture in order to learn what God has revealed about his character and conduct.[2] However, a critically important, if sometimes overlooked, part of the Christian vocation is recognizing false teachings, and learning how such teachings distort or contradict Christian faith. Christians with a limited knowledge of Scripture and the historic teachings of the Church, unaware of the existence or the dangers of false doctrines, may be easily led along paths that lead away from God. Thus, a key feature of this study is its identification and examination of teachings that are contrary to Scripture.

The Life of the Church *reflects* on how these texts and teachings can guide our life together as the body of Christ. The purpose of this section is to suggest ways in which the biblical teachings can shape our daily Christian life.

## Who could use these studies?

This study has been designed for use by a variety of individuals and groups. Some individuals might work straight through the entire study, writing out their answers to the discussion questions. Others may wish to study only selected lessons to learn more about specific aspects of God's character and conduct.

Beginning with this Introduction and the Table of Contents as an overview, this study could be used for a 13-week adult Sunday School course. A class that desires more time for discussion could expand this schedule by exploring The Text one week and The Teachings and The Life of the Church the next.

A session or board of deacons could use this study for their devotions. It would also provide a year-long study for Presbyterian Women, Presbyterian Men, or other organizations that meet monthly. Groups that meet nine times a year could combine some lessons in Parts II and III, or even skip Part III, to fit the material into their schedule. Study leaders should feel free to combine or divide lessons, adapting this resource to meet the needs of less formal Bible study gatherings.

Certainly the material presented in each lesson is far from exhaustive. The study leader who wishes to provide more background, or the study participant who wishes to explore the topics in more detail, will find a list of additional resources at the end of every lesson. Each lesson has been prepared so that it may be used "as is" or as a resource for a teacher preparing his or her own lesson plan.

## Why study what the Bible teaches about God?

"It is of great importance for Christian believers to have, from time to time, a reasonable, sane, mature person stand up in their midst and say 'God is ...' and go on to complete the sentence intelligently. ... The theologian offers his mind in the service of saying 'God' in such a way that God is not reduced or packaged or banalized, but known and contemplated and adored, with the consequence that our lives are not cramped into what we can explain but exalted by what we worship."[3]

It is my hope that these studies will speak to the mind as well as to the heart. Although we know the command "Love the Lord your God with all your heart and with all your soul and with all your *mind* and with all your strength" (Mark 12:30), the modern age tends to value feelings over facts. As a result, the modern church has been inclined to emphasize that which warms the heart over that which fires the mind. In response, I have looked to those who have offered their minds in the service of God, and have tried to draw together resources from throughout "the Great Tradition," which stretches back to the early church, through the Reformers and is continued in the best of current evangelical scholarship. For to strengthen our souls, we must nourish both our hearts and our minds.

It is my prayer that those who participate in this study – all of us by definition theologians, those who speak a word (*logos*) about God (*theos*) – will do so with the goal of more fully knowing, contemplating, and adoring the God whom alone we worship and serve.

### For Discussion

1. What benefits may Christians expect from studying what the Bible and the Church have to teach us about God?
2. What do you hope to learn through your participation in these studies?

# Additional resources

*The Doctrine of God: An Historical Survey*, Christopher B. Kaiser (Westchester, Ill.: Crossway, 1982).
> A helpful overview of the way God is revealed in the Old and New Testaments and the ways in which God has been understood throughout the history of the Church.

*The Christian Doctrine of God, One Being Three Persons*, Thomas F. Torrance (Edinburgh: T&T Clark, 1996).
> A thoroughly biblical, scholarly study "devoted to clarifying the understanding of the most profound article of the Christian Faith, the doctrine of the Holy Trinity," by one of this century's pre-eminent evangelical theologians.

*The Great Tradition: Evangelicals, Catholics & Orthodox in Dialogue*, James S. Cutsinger, ed., (Downers Grove: InterVarsity, 1997).
> Thought-provoking essays and responses on the foundational truths Christians hold in common across the dividing lines of time and denominations.

## Endnotes

1. "A Brief Statement of Faith" was adopted by the Presbyterian Church (USA) in 1991.
2. Scripture teaches, and the Church has always believed, that God is neither male nor female. As Lessons 3-7 illustrate, God's self-revelation includes a variety of names. To avoid numerous and cumbersome circumlocutions, this study guide will retain the historic language of Scripture and the Church in using the pronouns "he, his, himself" in reference to God.
3. Eugene Peterson, *Reversed Thunder: The Revelation of John and the Praying Imagination* (San Francisco: Harper and Row, 1988), pp. 3-4.

# In the Beginning, God

What were we made for? To know God.
What aim should we set ourselves in life? To know God.

*J.I. Packer*

## Overview

Genesis and the Gospel of John both begin by telling us what God has done. By describing God's nature and actions instead of debating the possibility of God's existence, these passages of Scripture offer us a model for our own study of God. They also teach us that our existence is not the accidental product of an impersonal process, but the intended result of the God who loves us, who creates, sustains and redeems us. This knowledge assures us that our lives have order, purpose and meaning.

### *Read: Genesis 1:1 and John 1:1-3*

### *For Discussion*

*1. In what ways are you creative? What are some things you have "created?" How have you felt about your creations?*

*2. What do these verses reveal to us about the existence and activity of God?*

# The Texts

## *Genesis 1:1*

Perhaps more has been written about Genesis 1:1 than any other single verse of Scripture. And with good reason. These words are the beginning of God's written revelation, a revelation that progressively unfolds God's redemptive relationship with his creation. In Hebrew, the first three words of Genesis 1:1 are *bereshith bara elohim*, literally, "In the beginning/created/God." *Bereshith* and *bara* will be given special attention in this lesson. We will look at *elohim* in Lesson 5.[1]

### *In the beginning [bereshith] (v. 1)*

*Bereshith* comes from a Hebrew root meaning "head," and has as its principal meaning the first, or beginning, of a series. Given its context in this verse, and its consistent use throughout the Old Testament, the unmistakable implication is that "in the beginning," that is, before anything else existed, there was only God.[2]

For modern Christians this concept has become so familiar that we easily lose sight of how radically it differed from the beliefs of ancient peoples. Other religions in Old Testament times had "creation" stories. But those began with a deity rearranging some existing material. The ancient Jewish assertion that "in the beginning" there was only God dramatically and unmistakably distinguished their faith from all competing religions and philosophies.

Indeed, one might be inclined to wonder how the children of Abraham, who unlike the Greeks had no tradition of philosophical speculation, could have developed such a notion on their own.

### *created [bara] (v. 1)*

Having been made in the image of God, all people have the urge and ability to create. *Yasar*, one of two Hebrew verbs that may be translated "create," emphasizes the shaping of an object. This is the sense in which human beings "create" such things as space shuttles and symphonies, dinners and dining room tables. *Bara*, however, stresses the initiation of the object. Throughout the Old Testament, *bara* in this grammatical form refers exclusively to God's creative activity. As a purely theological term, it points beyond human ability to divine activity.

## John 1:1-3

Concerned to convey eternal realities, yet constrained by the limits of human language, John penned one of the most poetic and profound passages of Scripture as the prologue to his gospel (1:1-18). From his first three verses, which intend primarily to introduce the life and work of Jesus, we also learn about the relational nature of God's eternal existence, and about the Word's role in creation.

### In the beginning [arche] was the Word [logos] (v. 1)

In an unmistakable allusion to Genesis 1:1, John writes about the origin of the universe. The word order of the sentence places the emphasis on "In the beginning." The Greek *arche*, here translated "beginning," often connotes "origin," which seems to be John's intent.

Commenting on these verses Karl Barth writes, "Only God, the Creator himself, was 'in the beginning.' ... His being ... is not temporal; it is the eternal being that in principle precedes and encloses and originates all time."[3] God, in other words, stands outside of time.

The idea that time itself is a part of God's creation can be difficult to grasp. But it is foundational to Christian faith that apart from our space-time universe, which came into being at his command, God eternally exists.

### Through him all things were made (v. 3)

"In the beginning," that is, before anything was created, the Word (*logos*) already was. Now John adds that the Word, Jesus Christ, was God's agent of creation, the "originator" of all things.

Combined with the mention of "the spirit of God" in Gen. 1:2, this reference to Christ as creator reveals that God has always existed as a Trinity of Father, Son, and Holy Spirit. While this study focuses on God the Father, our explorations of God's nature and activity must never lose sight of God's eternal triunity.

---

## For Discussion

1. What does the phrase "In the beginning," as used in Genesis and John, teach us about God?

2. What can creation tell us about the Creator? When have you been especially drawn toward the Creator by experiencing the creation?

3. What important things can creation not tell us about the Creator? What is needed to keep us from worshiping creation rather than the Creator?

---

# The Teachings

Two key teachings that emerge from these passages are that God has always existed and that God freely created out of nothing all else that now exists.

## God's eternal self-existence

It seems that at some point, every child asks, "Where did I come from?" Not content with any answer, many keep on asking, "Well, then who made ..." until they get to "So who made God?" Parents, understandably, may be inclined to answer "That's a very good question. Why don't you ask the minister next Sunday?" R.C. Sproul responds,

"God does not require a cause. He causes all creatures to be, but he himself is caused by no one. ... God exists by his own power. He alone is self-existent. Aseity, meaning 'self-existent,' is the characteristic that separates Him from all other things."[4]

While the term *aseity* (pronounced ah-SAY-ih-tee) may seem exotic, the concept it conveys – God's unique, eternal, uncreated existence – is childlike in its simplicity. No one made God. God always has been. That is part of what it means to say that God is God.

More complicated explanations of God's eternal existence have also been offered. Four classic arguments include:

1) *The Ontological Argument.* As formulated by Anselm of Canterbury in the 11th century, this "argument from being" defines God as "a being than which nothing greater can be conceived." Since that which exists in reality is greater than that which exists only in thought, if we can conceive of God he must therefore exist in reality. For Anselm, and those who offer modern variations on this theme, the very concept of God makes God's non-existence impossible.

2) *The Cosmological Argument.* In this "first cause" argument, Thomas Aquinas and others have pointed out that nothing in the world necessarily exists; nor is anything, even the world itself, the cause of its own existence. Rather, the existence of the world is contingent, that is, its existence depends on something (or Someone) other than itself, a reality that in turn necessarily exists. As Aquinas put it, "it is necessary to admit a first cause, to which everyone gives the name of God."

3) *The Teleological Argument.* Also known as the argument from design, in its simplest form this argument asserts that the universe shows evidence of both design and purpose. It appears to have been ordered for the sake of achieving a particular end. Evidence of design is thus evidence of a Designer, namely God. Aquinas framed this argument, "some intelligent being exists by whom all natural things are directed to their end; and this being we call God." A con-

temporary physicist similarly observes, "The more I examine the universe and the details of its architecture, the more evidence I find that the universe in some sense must have known we were coming."[5]

4) *The Moral Argument.* This argument is particularly associated with the 18th-century German philosopher Immanuel Kant, who held that all human beings feel an obligation, a "categorical imperative," to choose among certain values. For Kant, there could be no other possible explanation for this universal phenomenon than the existence of God, who is the source of moral law and the highest good.[6]

None of these arguments individually, nor all of them together, constitutes a rigorous mathematical "proof" of God's existence. Were human beings able to construct such a proof, we would have reduced God to our level. Neither are these intellectual exercises, valuable as they are, sufficient to generate faith in God. As Pascal rightly observed, reason and faith are of different orders.[7] (See Heb. 11:3.)

However, by using philosophy's own methods to answer philosophical concerns about the possibility of God's existence, these and similar arguments help show that historic Christian faith is not unreasonable. Therefore, such logical arguments can be useful for those wrestling with doubts that occasionally trouble even the most faithful Christians.

## Creatio ex nihilo

The doctrine *creatio ex nihilo*, literally "creation out of nothing," is "a relational idea. It affirms the absolute transcendence of God in relation to the world and the dependence of the world in relation to God. It makes no sense to imagine an actual 'nothing' out of which God made the world."[8]

The historic Christian teaching finds support from a surprising direction – modern science. The consensus among cosmologists, who study the origins of the universe, is that the visible (and invisible) universe began at an identifiable instant, dubbed the Big Bang, some 12 to 20 billion years ago. Many atheistic scientists now acknowledge what Jews and Christians have claimed for millennia – that the universe had a definite beginning.

As with philosophical arguments, scientific studies do not "prove" that God exists, or that God, as the instigator of the Big Bang, is the creator of the universe. John Polkinghorne, a physicist and Anglican priest, warns, "claims that modern physics has provided its own version of creation *ex nihilo* completely miss the point." For while physics may discover laws that would explain the appearance of a universe, "theology is concerned with the Giver of those laws, which are the basis of any form of physical reality."[9]

Science can go back only as far as the beginning of the universe. Such questions as "Why does this, or any, universe exist rather than none at all?" can only be answered by those who accept the biblical revelation that "In the beginning, God created the heavens and the earth."

## *For Discussion*

1. What questions do you remember asking about God when you were a child? Have those questions changed? Have they been answered?

2. Which of the four classic arguments for God's existence seems least compelling to you? Why? Which seems most compelling? Why?

3. What common grounds do philosophical discussions and scientific discoveries offer Christians for talking to non-Christians about the existence of God?

4. What is the significance of the historic Christian teaching of *creatio ex nihilo*?

# The Life of the Church

"When we understand from Genesis 1:1 that in the beginning *God is*, we have a lens for viewing all life, whether we are looking at the world outside or trying to see into ourselves. ... The conviction that *God is* affects all that we are and do."[10]

That the Bible does not try to prove God's existence does not mean that such scientific or philosophical exercises have no place in Christian faith and life. Philosophical arguments and scientific discoveries, human reason and experience play important roles in our knowledge of God. But such roles are always subordinate to God's self-revelation. The Bible's emphasis on God's eternal existence and free acts of creation reminds us that we know God only because God has made himself known.

The opening verses of Genesis and John teach us that we are not the random result of a biochemical process that inexplicably began several billion years ago. They remind us that God was not obligated to create the universe, and that there is no reason why this or any universe must exist. These passages assure us that from "before" the beginning of time, God – Father, Son, and Holy Spirit, eternally in relationship with one another – had a plan to create, sustain, and redeem humanity.

In a world that often seems chaotic and pointless, where scientists declare that the visible universe is all that ever was or will be, a world where philosophers wearily conclude that human life is of no ultimate significance, the knowledge that we were created and are loved by God assures us that our lives have order, purpose, and meaning.

As the Danish philosopher and theologian Sören Kierkegaard has rightly said, "To stand on one leg and prove God's existence is a very different thing from going down on one's knee and thanking him."

## For Discussion

1. Why can philosophy and science never prove (or disprove) the existence of God?

2. How might our study of these passages of Scripture and philosophical arguments influence our own faith? Our sharing our faith with other Christians? Our sharing our faith with non-Christians?

3. In what ways can the language of science and the calculations of mathematics be employed as songs of praise to God?

4. What difference does it make to know that you are God's creation, not the result of a random process?

## For reflection and response

Recall a time when the words of Scripture or a hymn combined with your being outdoors amidst creation to give you a strong sense of who the Creator is.

Pray and give God thanks for his good creation. You may wish to pray Psalm 19, or to use that psalm as a model for your prayer.

## Additional Resources

*Philosophy for Understanding Theology*, Diogenes Allen (Atlanta: John Knox Press, 1985).

The 15-page introduction, "The Foundation of Christian Theology: *The World Was Created*," offers a superb overview of the main themes of this lesson, and is a concise introduction to theology as a discipline.

*Theism, Atheism and Big Bang Cosmology*, William Lane Craig and Quentin Smith (Oxford: Clarendon Press, 1993).

A series of 12 essays by two philosophers debating the theological significance (or insignificance) of space and time beginning at the moment of the Big Bang. Alternating between Craig, an evangelical Christian, and Smith, an atheist, these occasionally technical essays provide significant and stimulating insight into questions about God and the beginning of the universe.

*God, Reason & Theistic Proofs*, Stephen T. Davis (Grand Rapids: Eerdmans, 1997).
Davis, a Presbyterian minister and professor of philosophy, explains how theistic proofs are constructed and what they can, and cannot, accomplish, and then examines classic arguments for God's existence.

*The Trinitarian Faith: The Evangelical Theology of the Ancient Catholic Church*, Thomas F. Torrance (Edinburgh: T&T Clark, 1993).
Reflecting on the Nicene Creed, Torrance gives special emphasis to God as Creator and the Triunity of God.

# Endnotes

1. Here, as throughout these lessons, the original language of the biblical text yields important insights into the meaning and application of the verses being studied.
2. Attempts to translate *bereshith* as "when" rather than "in the beginning," while grammatically possible, may be motivated less by linguistic considerations than the desire to make Genesis conform to the phrase *enuma elish*, "When on high," which begins the Babylonian creation epic.
3. Karl Barth, *Witness to the Word: A Commentary on John 1* (Grand Rapids: Eerdmans, 1986), p. 20.
4. R.C. Sproul, *One Holy Passion* (Nashville: Thomas Nelson, 1987), pp. 15-16.
5. Freeman Dyson, *Disturbing the Universe* (San Francisco: Harper & Row, 1979), p. 256.
6. A more accessible and unabashedly Christian form of this argument is offered by C.S. Lewis in *Mere Christianity* (New York: Macmillan, 1943).
7. For a discussion of these orders see pp. 32-51 of Diogenes Allen's *Three Outsiders* (Cambridge, Mass: Cowley Publications, 1983).
8. Christopher B. Kaiser, *The Doctrine of God* (Westchester, Ill: Crossway Books, 1982), p. 49.
9. John Polkinghorne, *The Faith of A Physicist* (Princeton: Princeton University Press, 1995), p. 10.
10. Bruce Larson, *My Creator, My Friend* (Waco: Word, 1986), p. 17.

# Making All Things New

From Thee, great God, we spring, to Thee we tend –
Path, motive, guide, original and end.
*Boethius*

## Overview

In Lesson 1 we looked to the first verse of the Bible and the first verses of John's gospel to see what God's creation of heaven and earth revealed to us about God's being and activity. In this lesson we turn to Mark's gospel and the last book of the Bible to learn about God's ultimate plans for creation. What we learn from Mark is that God is willing to pay an unimaginable price to redeem us from our slavery to sin and thereby to restore unbroken fellowship with his human creation. What we find in Revelation is not an ending, as we might expect, but a glorious new beginning.

---

*Read: Mark 10:45 and Revelation 21:1-5*

### For Discussion

*1. When you know the ending before you begin, how does that knowledge affect your reading of a story or viewing of a movie?*

*2. How does it affect your daily Christian life to know "the end of the story" even though we're living "in the middle?"*

# The Texts

## Mark 10:45

After an unseemly argument among his disciples, Jesus reminds them that he has come not to be served, but to give his own life so that people may be freed from their slavery to sin and restored to fellowship with God.

### *the Son of Man ... [came] to give his life as a ransom for many (10:45)*

This verse "is foundational to the New Testament doctrine of redemption ... The imagery implies that we are held in a captivity from which only the payment of a ransom can set us free, and that the ransom is nothing less than the Messiah's own life."[1]

God's will and work to redeem his people is a central theme of Scripture. Throughout the Old and New Testaments God is identified as the redeemer of his people. Isaiah prophesies, "This is what the LORD says – your Redeemer, the Holy One of Israel: 'I am the LORD your God, who teaches you what is best for you, who directs you in the way you should go'" (Isa. 48:17). And Paul writes of our waiting "for the blessed hope – the glorious appearing of our great God and Savior, Jesus Christ, who gave himself for us to redeem us from all wickedness" (Titus 2:13-14).

The book of Revelation grants a glimpse of this redeemed community of faith.

## Revelation 21:1-5

Revelation is one of the most studied books of the Bible, yet it is perhaps the least understood. Its language is saturated with that of the Old Testament, although it never directly quotes a single Old Testament text. As Eugene Peterson notes, "It is generally agreed that the Revelation has to do with eschatology, that is, with 'last things.' What is frequently missed is that all the eschatology is put to immediate pastoral use. Eschatology is the most pastoral of all the theological perspectives, showing how the ending impinges on the present in such ways that the truth of the gospel is verified in life 'in the middle.'"[2]

By showing us the last things as a new beginning, these verses shed light on the character and conduct of God, our creator and redeemer, our source and our goal. For those of us living "in the middle," this pastoral perspective helps us see Revelation as a wonderfully practical resource for our daily faith and life.

### Then I saw a new heaven and a new earth (v. 1)

Although the Bible frequently mentions the new heaven and the new earth (see Isa. 65:17; 66:22; Ps. 102:25f.; II Pet. 3:13), it gives few details about what they will be like. We are, however, assured that the new heaven and new earth will differ dramatically from what we now know. The Greek word here translated "new" conveys the sense of being new in character as well as recently made. It further implies a qualitative contrast with that which is old: The old is obsolete, the new is dramatically superior. This same word is used in Hebrews 8:8-13 (which quotes Jer. 31:31-34), "The time is coming, declares the Lord, when I will make a *new* covenant with the house of Israel and with the house of Judah. ... "

All of us, at times, look forward to a day when our lives will be more tranquil and fulfilling than they seem at the moment. Perhaps Scripture leaves the new heaven and new earth largely undescribed because our limited human experiences and imagination are utterly unable to envision the newness of life God has planned for us.

### Now the dwelling of God is with men (v. 3)

Living in an intimate relationship with another person is a deeply rooted human desire. Here John's vision again recalls the prophecy of Jeremiah 31, and speaks to that desire by using the term "dwelling," a word that conveys overtones of God's covenant with his chosen people.

Throughout Scripture God's dwelling is associated with fellowship and blessing. In the Old Testament, the dwelling place of God was first the tabernacle in the wilderness, then the temple in Jerusalem. With the coming of Christ, God took up temporary dwelling among humanity, as "the Word became flesh and dwelt among us" (John 1:14, RSV). Christians now "know that we live in [God] and he in us, because he has given us of his Spirit" (I John 4:13). And in the age to come, our faith will be changed to sight, and the servants of God "will see his face" (Rev. 22:4).

Unhindered fellowship between God and his people, seeing God's face, is the goal of God's redemption of creation. All the promises of God's covenant – made first to Abraham, renewed through Moses, and embodied in Christ – will be fully realized when God dwells among his redeemed people in the new heaven and new earth.

## There will be no more death or mourning or crying or pain (v. 4)

Another dramatic difference between the old earth and the new will be the absence of death. The decay, diseases, and disasters that are such prominent features of our present lives simply will not exist in the new heaven and new earth. The grief and pain so frequently connected with the separation caused by death will be at most distant memories.

The abolition of death, described in Revelation 20, is a blessing that will flow from our uninterrupted communion with God. In the new heaven and earth, "all the evils that have burdened and cursed human existence will flee from the presence of God."[3] Crying and pain, mourning and death resulted from human sin. In the new heaven and new earth, these consequences of our separation from God by sin will be no more. Christ will have conquered every enemy, including the "last enemy," death (I Cor. 15:19-26).

*"I am making everything new!" (v. 5)*

The newness introduced in vv. 1-4 reaches its climax in v. 5 with God's promise to make "everything new." Such making new, or re-creation, is a frequent biblical image of salvation (see Isa. 65:17-25; II Pet. 3:1-13). Indeed, Paul assures us that God has already begun making everything new through the work of Jesus Christ: "if anyone is in Christ, he is a new creation" (II Cor. 5:17). The completion of God's ultimate re-creation of the heavens and the earth awaits Christ's triumphant return and his final victory over death and sin.

*Write this down, for these words are trustworthy and true (v. 5)*

It is characteristic of God that all that God says is "trustworthy" (from the Greek root for the word faith, meaning "certain, reliable") and "true" (correct, dependable, in conformity to the facts). These same two adjectives are used of Jesus Christ in Revelation 3:14 and again in 19:11. Many people have written many words about the end times. Much of what has been written has proved untrue. But what God has revealed, what he told John to write down for our instruction and encouragement, is unquestionably trustworthy and undeniably true.

## *For Discussion*

1. What in this world causes you to yearn for God to make everything new?

2. How is knowing the ending of the story important to our living now, in the middle of it?

3. How does the prophecy in Jeremiah 31:31-34 relate to John's vision in Revelation 21:1-5? What is the connection between a new heart and the new heaven and new earth?

# The Teachings

Two key teachings found within these verses are that God never ceases to care for what he has created and that God's eternal plan is to redeem his chosen people, and so restore their unmediated fellowship with him.

## *God continues to care for his fallen creation.*

One of the most comforting of all Christian doctrines is that God did not abandon his human creation after they rejected him by disobeying his command.

Although Eve and Adam sinned, and although as a consequence they suffered pain, banishment from Eden, and eventually death, still God did not leave his people entirely dependent on their own resources, "The LORD God made garments of skin for Adam and his wife and clothed them" (Gen. 3:21). Despite their rebellion, God continued to care for those who willfully disobeyed his command.

Similarly, the people of Israel repeatedly abandoned the God who had delivered them from slavery in Egypt. They worshiped a golden calf, clamored for a king, ignored God's law, and persecuted his prophets, yet God still heard and answered their prayers for deliverance from the difficulties caused by their own disobedience. God's redeeming love for his rebellious people was so great "that he gave his one and only Son, that whoever believes in him shall not perish but have eternal life" (John 3:16). God's continuing concern for his people is shown by the present work of the Holy Spirit (see John 14:16-17, 26; 16:7-15; Rom. 8:26-27).

The biblical revelation of God's ongoing involvement with creation contrasts sharply with a belief system known as "deism." Deism acknowledges the existence of a divine being, and accepts that deism's "god" created the universe, but holds that this creator has no ongoing contact with the world. Deism flourished in late

17th- and 18th-century England, influencing thinkers who are still influential today, perhaps most notably German philosopher Immanuel Kant. Moreover, many today subscribe (often unknowingly) to a variation of this belief system, accepting the existence of a deity as creator of the universe while rejecting the God revealed in Scripture, a God who continues to interact with his creation.

### *God has eternally planned to redeem his people.*

Anyone who has been through, or watched loved ones endure, the pain of a divorce or the death of a child knows how deeply a severed relationship can wound the human soul. God knows this pain as well. From before the creation of time, God planned to be in fellowship with his people. Human sin interrupted that relationship. To redeem people from their captivity to sin, and eternal separation from him, God sent his only Son as our Redeemer.

Through his incarnation, sinless life, death, and resurrection, Jesus Christ healed our sin-severed fellowship with God and rescued us from death. This is the doctrine of the Atonement – the historic Christian teaching that God himself became incarnate (enfleshed) in Jesus Christ so that sinful human beings might again be "at-one" with their Creator. While Christians may debate the precise nature of the Atonement, those who today deny any need for any form of this foundational Christian doctrine misunderstand the effects of sin, the holiness of God, and the unwavering love God lavishes on his rebellious human creation.

The ultimate benefits of the Atonement, the point at which we will dwell in the unmediated presence of God, can only be experienced "when the times will have reached their fulfillment." Through the present ministry of the Holy Spirit and our fellowship with other Christians, we have a foretaste, a down payment, of that restored relationship. Such glimpses of heaven, especially when combined with visions of the new heaven and new earth, increase our desire to enter ever more completely into God's presence.

> **For Discussion**
>
> 1. How does deism's god differ from the God revealed in Scripture?
> 2. What are some ways in which you have seen God's active involvement in the world today? In your own life?
> 3. What makes the Atonement necessary?
> 4. How has God chosen to heal the broken fellowship between himself and his creation?

# The Life of the Church

God's pain at being separated from us by our sin is so deep that God the Son became incarnate to restore the relationship. As Mark's gospel shows us, God's love for us is so great that he sent his beloved Son to give his life as a ransom for our sins.

John's vision of a new heaven and a new earth, while concerned with last things, also helps us learn about the God whom we worship and serve as we live "in the middle," that is, in the time between creation and creation's final redemption; in the time between God's speaking into existence the heavens and the earth and the coming of the new heaven and the new earth.

Jesus' assertion that he has come as our redeemer, and John's vision of God dwelling with us and wiping every tear from our eyes, reassure us that our God is a God who has forever planned to care for us throughout eternity. The more we know about the nature and character of God, the greater our desire to develop an increasingly intimate relationship with him, a redeemed relationship in which we move closer to God and allow God to draw ever nearer to us.

Our desire for a redeemed relationship with God, for an increasing awareness of God's habitual presence, draws us to meditate on what it will be like to spend eternity with him. Or, to approach this topic from the opposite direction, "If we don't want God, or don't want him very near, we can hardly be expected to be very interested in heaven."[4]

## For Discussion

1. How could the promise of a new creation influence the way we approach daily life? What hope does it provide in the midst of our suffering?

2. How do we experience our redemption in our daily Christian life?

3. What do these verses reveal about the existence and activities of God that we could share with others?

## For reflection and response

Recall ways in which you have seen the new creation of God provide hope and comfort in your life. Describe ways you have seen people enter into the new creation and actually change they way they were living.

Pray and give God thanks for the promise of the new creation. You may wish to pray Psalm 30, or to use this psalm as a model for your prayer.

## Additional Resources

*The Actuality of Atonement*, Colin E. Gunton  (Edinburgh: T&T Clark, 1988).
   A contemporary study of the Atonement that approaches the doctrine by way of considering the nature of speech about God.

*Reversed Thunder: The Revelation of John and the Praying Imagination*, Eugene Peterson (San Francisco: Harper & Row, 1988).
> Not a verse-by-verse commentary, but a uniquely helpful thematic approach to the Revelation and its immediate applicability to the Christian's daily life.

## Endnotes

1. John R.W. Stott, *The Cross of Christ* (Downer's Grove: InterVarsity Press, 1986), p. 177.
2. Eugene Peterson, *Reversed Thunder: The Revelation of John and the Praying Imagination* (San Francisco: Harper & Row, 1988), p. 9.
3. George Eldon Ladd, *A Commentary on the Revelation of John* (Grand Rapids: Eerdmans, 1972), p. 279.
4. Peterson, *Reversed Thunder*, p. 185.

# I AM WHO I AM

God is truth, and light His shadow.
*Plato*

## Overview

Throughout the Old Testament there is a close connection between a person's name and character. Consider Abram's name being changed to Abraham (meaning "father of a multitude"); the wily Jacob bearing a name that means "he supplants"; and the widowed, sonless Naomi (meaning pleasant) telling the people of Bethlehem to call her Mara (meaning bitter). This lesson, the first of five to explore the names of God, focuses on the divine name, I AM WHO I AM, and shows how God's revelation of his name is inseparable from God's commission to his people to make his name known.

---

*Read: Exodus 3:13-15*

*For Discussion*

*1. What comes to your mind when you hear the name of someone you know?*

*2. What do we learn about God's existence and God's character from his revelation of his name to Moses?*

# The Text

## *Exodus 3:13-15*

At the outset of Exodus 3 (a passage we will study in Lesson 11), Moses was tending his father-in-law's flock when he saw a bush that "was blazing, yet it was not consumed." There God told Moses that he had chosen him to lead the Israelites out of slavery in Egypt. As Moses stood on that holy ground, he tried to escape this unexpected and unwanted calling by raising questions. In response to one of these questions, God revealed his name to Moses.

### *If ... they ask me, "What is his name?" (v. 13)*

Most of us would be nervous (to say the least) if we were unexpectedly appointed to lead a rebellion against a powerful ruler. Understandably anxious about his unsought commission, Moses expresses his personal doubts in terms of an anticipated question from his people, "What is his name?"

While that may seem an unusual, or even irrelevant, question to us, it would have been of critical importance to Moses and the ancient Israelites, for "In Old Testament times a name expressed identification, but also identity. ... Names had an explanatory function ... Scripture makes much of the name for deity because in the name lies a theology."[1] Since learning God's name would offer insight into God's character, this request (whether from the Israelites or Moses) effectively asks God to reveal something of his nature.

Of course, Moses can tell the Israelites nothing more than God has told him. He can know no more of God than God is willing to reveal. So while God's answer does not sanction or condemn Moses' doubts, neither, one suspects, does it fully satisfy his curiosity.

It is also important to recognize that this revelation of the divine name is directly connected to Moses' commission. God did not reveal his name so that Moses could stay in the desert and keep this knowledge to himself. Instead, it was to equip Moses for his calling that God answered "I AM WHO I AM."

## I AM WHO I AM (v. 14)

In ancient Hebrew, the earliest written form of which did not use vowels, the name God revealed to Moses is rendered by the consonants YHWH. Earlier translators thought "Jehovah" was the best way to bring this word into English. However, most scholars now agree that "Yahweh" is more accurate.

This name is the most frequent term for God in the Old Testament, occurring more than 5,000 times. It is found in every Old Testament book except Ecclesiastes and Esther. Scripture speaks of Yahweh as "this glorious and awesome name" (Deut. 28:58) and simply "*the* name" (Lev. 24:11). Yahweh is "my Rock and my Redeemer" (Ps. 19:14). In contrast to *elohim* (see Lesson 4), a name that speaks of God's transcendence, the name Yahweh conveys God's immanence, his closeness to and concern for his human creation, and his revelation of his redemptive covenant.[2]

Scholars continue to debate the origin of the name YHWH. Some suggest it comes from a Semitic root meaning "to fall" or "to blow"; thus the God who causes rain (or enemies) to fall, or the one who causes wind to blow. Others trace it to the Ugaritic word for "word"; thus the God who reveals himself in a word. The most widely accepted explanation is that Yahweh is a form of the Hebrew verb "to be, to become"; thus the God who is or who will be: The Eternal One. This is the sense conveyed in most English translations, "I AM WHO I AM."

While some still search for ways to explain God's name as mere human invention, "An alternative solution is to take seriously Israel's own tradition [which] emphasizes the newness of the name to Moses."[3]

## the God of Abraham ... Isaac and ... Jacob (v. 15)

No matter how well we know the stories of God's presence in

the lives of his people, no individual or group can ever know all there is to know of God. "Yahweh" had always been God's name. But while God had always been Yahweh (see Ex. 6:3), Abraham, Isaac, and Jacob had known him through his revelatory deeds as *el-shaddai* (God Almighty). It was not until his call to Moses at the burning bush that God identified himself by this name to his people.

This gracious act of self-revelation reminds us that no matter how long we (or our families) have been members of a particular church, God remains able to make himself personally present to us in ways we could never imagine.

### *This is my name forever (v. 15)*

God's answer to Moses' question was not an off-the-cuff response, such as a distracted parent might give to a pestering child. Rather, in telling Moses that Yahweh "is my name forever," God helps us see that the implications of this revelation extend far beyond Moses' question. God revealed to Moses his eternal name, the name that would be remembered by God's people throughout all future generations. As one commentator observes, "The revelation of the name in Israel is not to satisfy curiosity, but to be the medium of continuous worship."[4]

## For Discussion

1. Why was it so important to Moses that he learn God's name? What can contemporary Christians learn from God's answer to Moses' question?

2. At what places in your life have you felt the desire to know more about the nature of God?

3. Why do you think God revealed himself to Moses as *Yahweh* after revealing himself to the patriarchs as *el-shaddai*?

# The Teachings

Two key teachings that emerge from these passages are that God is a person, not a projection, and that God reveals himself to us.

## *God is a person*

Whether YHWH comes from the Hebrew root word "to be" or stands completely apart from any linguistic derivation, this name emphasizes God's eternal self-existence and his self-determination. While no single self-revelation completely encompasses the fullness of God, in revealing this name to Moses God does show that he is not just a philosophical notion or mere psychological projection, but a person who desires to be known by name. "I am the LORD [*YHWH*]; that is my name! I will not give my glory to another or my praise to idols" (Isa. 42:8).

"The centrality of God's personality is seen in the fact that while he is the Creator and Preserver of all nature, he is encountered in Scripture not primarily as the God of nature, as in pagan religions, but rather as the God of history, controlling and directing the affairs of man. The central place of the covenant by which he links himself in a personal relationship to men is further indication of the scriptural emphasis on the personal nature of God."[5]

We must beware the temptation to consider the "personhood" of God as some cosmic extension of the human individual. The truth, as Genesis 1 makes clear, is that our human personhood is a finite representation, an image, of the personhood of God. As Karl Barth has written, "It follows from the trinitarian understanding of God revealed in the Scripture that this one God is to be understood not just as impersonal lordship, i.e., as power, but as the Lord; not just as absolute Spirit but as Person, i.e., as an *I* existing in and for himself with his own thought and will. This is how He meets us in His revelation."[6]

Because God is a person, we are able, by his grace, to enter into a personal relationship with him. Modernity may tell us that God is merely projection of our inner wants and needs (the psychological approach) or a hypothesis invented to explain the otherwise inexplicable (the scientific or philosophical approach). However, the God who revealed himself to Moses through the burning bush is neither the product of human minds nor the projection of human hopes and fears. Rather, the God whom alone Christians worship and serve is a God who knows our names, and who makes himself known to us by revealing his name.

## God reveals himself to us

Decisions about where, how, and to whom he chooses to reveal himself are expressions of God's personhood. When God made himself known through Moses he did so from a burning bush by telling Moses his name. One lesson we can learn from this act is that since we did not name God, it is not our prerogative to rename, recreate, or re-imagine God to suit our present purposes.

This is of critical importance because there are those today who insist on discarding God's self-revelation, in place of which they substitute names and figures they themselves have created. However, "Since God alone defines the nature and being of God, God alone is possessed of the "right" to "name" (in the sense of "define") God. Human beings, whether male or female, have no "right" to name God. Given that God is *real* in the strictest sense of the word imaginable, the criterion of the adequacy of a theology will be the extent to which that which it says of God corresponds to the Reality God has determined Himself to be."[7]

As we cannot completely comprehend all that the name "Yahweh" conveys, so we must recognize that no single name for God completely captures or carries the reality of God. We must also realize that what God has revealed of himself is sufficient for us to come to a saving knowledge of him. When God revealed his name to Moses from the burning bush it was not so that Moses, ancient Israelites, or modern seekers would have the answers to all their questions about his character and conduct. Rather, this giving of the divine name must be seen in the light of the commission to Moses – leaving the desert, going to the people, and telling them "I AM has sent me to you."

## For Discussion

1. What do we learn about God's personhood from his self-revelation as YHWH?

2. What difference does it make in our daily lives to know God as a person rather than as a force or projection?

3. Is it possible for human beings to learn about God apart from God's self-revelation? Why (and how) or why not?

4. Why might people be tempted to reduce God to a psychological projection or philosophical conjecture? What appears to be gained? What is lost?

# The Life of the Church

Moses was reluctant to tell his people, not to mention Pharaoh, that God had chosen him to lead the people of Israel out of Egypt and into the Promised Land. That is understandable. Being thrust into a leadership position for the purpose of challenging a powerful ruler would certainly unnerve most of us. Indeed, we are at times reluctant to share what God has taught with those we know, love, and trust. And yet, Yahweh has chosen each of us – just as surely as he chose the Apostles and Moses and Abraham – to be among the ones called to make his name known. The commissioning of Moses at the burning bush helps us see the connection between the revelation and the proclamation of God's name.

Before speaking to Moses at the burning bush, God had revealed himself to individuals, most notably to Abraham, Isaac, and Jacob. Here God reveals himself through an individual (Moses) to a people (Israel). God makes his name known to Moses so that Moses might make the name "Yahweh" known to God's people. Centuries later God revealed himself supremely in Jesus Christ, God Incarnate, who became flesh and dwelt among us. (See John 1:1-18.) Whenever God reveals himself – whether to Moses through the burning bush, to disciples in Galilee, or to those of us who follow him today – it is always so that those who know God's name may make him known to others.

Moses asked God how he should respond if the Israelites asked of him "What is his name?" God's answer, I AM WHO I AM, "reveals God's nature in the highest and fullest sense possible. It includes, or presupposes, the meaning of the other names. Yahweh particularly stresses the absolute faithfulness of God. God had promised the patriarchs that he would be their God, that he would be with them, would deliver and bless them, keep them, and give them a land as a place of service and inheritance.

"Moses is told by God that Israel is about to behold and experience the unchangeableness of God as he steadfastly and wondrously remembers his word and executes it to the fullest degree. God would prove to be a faithful, redeeming, upholding, restoring God. In working out this redemption, God would demonstrate that he is all that his name implies: merciful, gracious, patient, full of loving-kindness, truthful, faithful, forgiving, just, and righteous."[8]

God is still known by that name today. And it is still our commission to make that name known.

## For Discussion

1. Have you ever found yourself unexpectedly assuming a leadership position? In what ways did God help you in that situation?

2. What are the concerns underlying Moses' question, "What is his name?" How does God handle similar doubts and fears that we bring to him?

3. In Jesus, God has both a face and a name. How does that affect the way we tell others about him?

4. What are some ways in which we can carry out God's commission to make his name known?

## For reflection and response

Recall a time when you have been reluctant to do something God has called you to do. How did you respond? Is there any part of that response you would change if you were presented with a similar call today?

Pray and give God thanks that he is who he is. You may wish to pray Psalm 138, or to use that psalm as a model for your prayer.

## Additional Resources

*From Stone Age to Christianity: Monotheism and the Historical Process*, William F. Albright (Baltimore: Johns Hopkins Press, 1940).
A classic study on the development of the doctrine of God.

*The Christian Doctrine of God, One Being Three Persons*, Thomas F. Torrance (Edinburgh: T&T Clark, 1996).
Not easy reading, but very rewarding. Chapter 5, "One Being, Three Persons," offers especially helpful insights into the nature of God as a personal being and the meaning of the name *YHWH*.

# Endnotes

1. Elmer A Martens, "God, Names of" in *Evangelical Dictionary of Biblical Theology* (Grand Rapids: Baker, 1996), p. 297.
2. On God's immanence and transcendence, see Lesson 11.
3. Brevard Childs, *Exodus* (Philadelphia: Westminster Press, 1974), p. 64.
4. Childs, *Exodus*, p. 77.
5. R.L. Saucy, "God, Doctrine of" in *Evangelical Dictionary of Theology* (Grand Rapids: Baker, 1984), p. 462.
6. Karl Barth, *Church Dogmatics*, I.1 (Edinburgh: T&T Clark, 1975), p. 358.
7. Diogenes Allen, et al., "An Open Letter to Presbyterians: Theological Analysis of Issues Raised by the Re-imagining Conference" (unpublished, 1994), p. 6.
8. Gerard Van Groningen, "Names of God" in *Baker Encyclopedia of the Bible* (Grand Rapids: Baker, 1988), p. 884.

# No Other Gods

God is of no importance unless He is of supreme importance.
*Abraham Joshua Heschel*

## Overview

Unlike the "gods" worshiped by ancient peoples, the God who spoke to Moses from the burning bush and again from Mount Sinai is not one who keeps people guessing about who he is or what he expects of them. The God worshiped and served by Christians is one who reveals himself and his commandments to his people. Our proper response to God's redemptive revelation is to turn away from all other gods and to worship and serve God alone.

*Read: Exodus 20:1-3*

*For Discussion*

*1. What is the gift, and the warning, contained in this declaration?*

*2. What can we learn from these verses about God and God's commandments?*

# The Text

## *Exodus 20:1-3*

The people of Israel arrived at Mount Sinai three months after their exodus from Egypt. During their journey through the wilderness they had learned to lean on God's grace day by day. They had passed through the waters as God rescued them from certain annihilation at the Red Sea, collected the daily manna God provided for their food, and watched as water gushed out of a rock. Now all Israel trembled as "Mount Sinai was covered with smoke because the LORD descended on it in fire" (Ex. 19:18). Here, as God prepares to reveal what we now call the Ten Commandments, he identifies himself to his chosen people as *Yahweh elohim*, "the LORD your God."

## *And God spoke all these words [dabar] (v. 1)*

This introductory phrase serves as a preface to the whole law, not just the first commandment. It announces that the commands that follow are neither random nor capricious, but integrally connected to whom God has revealed himself to be.

The Hebrew *dabar* is translated 85 different ways in the King James Version of the Bible. Its primary sense, however, is "word," and "as 'word' *dabar* principally means what God said or says." The Ten Commandments, literally "the ten words" (Deut. 4:13; 10:4) are "the ten words (*debarim*) which the Lord spoke (*dibber*). ... The ten words are what God said; they are ten commandments because of how God said them."[1]

God's spoken word is a central feature of the Bible. In Genesis 1, God spoke, and the world came to be. In Exodus 3, he spoke his name from the burning bush, thereby revealing something of his character to Moses. Here he speaks to instruct his chosen people how to relate to him and to each other. Later "the word of the Lord" came to the prophets, forceful reminders to a forgetful people. Ultimately, "the Word became flesh and dwelt among us" (John 1:14, RSV).

### *I am the LORD [YHWH] your God [elohim] (v. 2)*

All that God will teach his people is rooted in the announcement: "I am Yahweh your God."

The Hebrew word here translated "God" is a form of *elohim*, a plural form of the generic Hebrew term for "deity." The plural is significant because it conveys the unity of the one God while allowing for the Trinity of persons found in Genesis 1:2 and in the New Testament. It is also noteworthy that the plural *elohim* has no parallels in other ancient Semitic languages, but occurs only in Hebrew.

*Elohim* is found more than 2,500 times in the Old Testament. When indicating the God of Israel, "*elohim* functions as the subject of all divine activity revealed to man and as the object of all true reverence and fear from men." As in this verse, it is often accompanied by the personal name of God, Yahweh. And *elohim* is often combined with descriptive terms to indicate the various titles by which God's people come to know him, for example, God of All the Earth (Isa. 54:5), Living God (Jer. 10:10), and God of Salvation (Ps. 18:46).[2]

### *who brought you out of the land of Egypt (v. 2)*

It is easy to idealize the past, even events from which we are not that far removed. Many of us tend to remember only the best. We conveniently forget painful or unpleasant memories. As the Exodus unfolds, Israel exemplifies this tendency.

Wandering in the wilderness, Israel soon forgot that Egypt was a land in which many gods were worshiped. In this verse, Yahweh reminds his people that he alone is Israel's Redeemer (see Lesson 2), the God who freed his people from their bondage to the cruel Egyptians and their harsh deities. This self-identification reminds Israel of God's right to make his will known to his people, on whose behalf he has already acted so graciously. The Ten Commandments, literally the "ten words," that God spoke to Israel at Sinai spell out God's standards for his covenant people, whom he freely delivered without demanding any prior commitment.

## *You shall have no other gods before me (v. 3)*

Many things can move almost unnoticed into a place between us and God. Other gods come in all shapes and sizes. Anything that threatens to consume our time and energy can become a contender for God's place. Unfortunately, the First Commandment has become so familiar that we may reflexively agree with what it says without pausing to consider what it means. Only by paying constant attention to this demanding word are we able to avoid slipping into the comfortable adoration of false gods that would come between us and the one true God whom alone we worship and serve.

When literally translated, this commandment begins in the singular, "*It* is not to be to you." This construction emphasizes the prohibition of associating with even one other god. ("You" is also singular, indicating that each individual member of the covenant community is specifically involved; there is no one for whom this expectation is invalid.) The grammar then switches to the plural "other gods" to make clear that the people of Israel are forbidden to associate with *any* potential deities. Among the Israelites, "The expression *other gods* became a regular, stereotyped term for the gods of the gentiles, who are no-gods. Every deity apart from the Lord is *another* god. The adjective *other* came to assume in Hebrew the signification of something strange or bizarre, something that is other than it should be."[3]

The use of the phrase "no other gods" does not mean that God acknowledged the existence of other deities, but that it was possible for Israel to choose to worship someone, or something, other than Yahweh. "Before me," literally "before my face" may also be translated "in defiance of me, to my disadvantage, over against me, so long as I exist."

What Yahweh made clear to those gathered at the foot of Mount Sinai was that he alone was to be Israel's God, to the exclusion of all other "gods" that the Israelites worshiped besides him in Egypt, and to which they repeatedly desired to return during the wilderness journey (See Josh. 24:14; Ezek. 20:5-10). This is foundational. Yahweh has given himself to Israel; they are to have no other gods in his place.

> ## For Discussion
>
> 1. What is the significance of the time and place at which God spoke "the ten words" to Israel?
> 2. Why was it important for God to remind his people that he had redeemed them from slavery in Egypt? How are we today reminded that God has redeemed us?
> 3. Why do you think God was so demanding of his people's allegiance?
> 4. What does the name *elohim* add to our knowledge of God?

# The Teachings

Two key teachings that emerge from these verses are the power and importance of God's spoken word and God's exclusive claim upon his people.

## God's spoken word

God is not a human invention, a literary fiction created to convey moral platitudes. The Eternal God reveals himself through his words to his people. Similarly, the Ten Commandments are not a Hebrew variation on a pre-existing Babylonian justice code. They are the words spoken by *Yahweh elohim*, the God who made the heavens and the earth, who revealed himself to the patriarchs and to Moses, who redeemed his people from slavery in Egypt.

The Ten Commandments are given in the context of the making of the covenant between *Yahweh elohim* and his people. This covenant implies a mutual obligation. The people are to obey his commands, which is another way of saying that they are to fulfill the terms of the covenant. In return, God agrees to treat them as his special possession, to make of them a kingdom of priests, a holy nation (Ex. 19:5-6). However, as Moses would later remind the people, "If you ever forget the LORD your God and follow other gods and worship and bow down to them, I testify against you today that you will surely be destroyed. Like the nations the LORD destroyed before you, so you will be destroyed for not obeying the LORD your God" (Deut. 8:19-20).

These commands of the covenant are absolute and unconditional, "which lifts them above all circumstances and every accident of detail."[4]

## God's exclusiveness

The first commandment does not say that there are no other gods, as does, for example, Isaiah. 45:21, "There is no God apart from me." Rather, the first commandment describes the relation of the people Israel to Yahweh their God, categorically eliminating any and all other gods as far as Israel is concerned.

"The first commandment is not an assertion of monotheistic conviction, that Yahweh is the only God, and hence the sole choice. The Old Testament makes very clear that such was not the case in the world of ancient Israel. The first commandment, in a sense, was called for by the many gods who demanded of Israel the allegiance Yahweh alone had the right to command. The commandment does not specify that no one is to have 'other gods,' but that *Israel* is to have no other gods."[5]

Modern Christians live in a setting not unlike that of ancient Israel. We too are surrounded by a culture that emphasizes religious and moral pluralism. The "gods" worshiped today, some old some new, are many and varied: money, power, prestige; sexual expression and personal experience; ancestors and Allah, Sophia and self. Against this rising tide of other gods, Christians are called to the steadfast worship and service of *Yahweh elohim*. As John J. Davis writes,

"The one thing that provided a cohesive force for the tribes of Israel was her worship of the true God. It was this truth that bound her together as one people. When she departed from this basic theological principle, confusion and frustration were the immediate results (see Judg. 17-18). The unity and growth of the tribes of Israel depended on the perpetuation of this theological principle."[6]

The unity and growth of contemporary Christians similarly depends on the worship of the God who revealed himself to Israel at Sinai.

## For Discussion

1. What does it teach us about the nature and character of God that he gathered his people together to speak directly to them?

2. What motivates us to look at something other than God to meet our needs?

3. Why has the temptation to worship other gods been so prevalent throughout the history of God's people? Are there any unique temptations that we face today that God's people have not faced in the past?

4. What is the importance of worship in our lives? Are there ways that our corporate and individual worship times could become more meaningful?

# The Life of the Church

The people of God have always had to struggle against the temptation to have and worship other gods. As the Israelites wandered through the desert, returning to worship the gods of Egypt remained a constant, and evidently compelling, option.

Our modern list of alternative deities may differ from that of the ancient Israelites, but our temptation to worship other gods is just as real. The first step toward disobeying the first commandment is accepting the currently fashionable notion that what the Bible and the Church call commandments are not the authoritative words of *Yahweh elohim* but simply the historically conditioned recommendations of well-meaning but quite fallible human beings. However, once we allow ourselves to be convinced that God has not spoken, we have placed another god, tangible or philosophical, before the face of God.

The close connection between the prohibition against other gods and the mandate to worship Yahweh alone is central to the faith and life of Israel. God's command that his people worship no other gods helps us see that Israel did not, as some presume, gradually progress to a belief in a single deity. Rather, that *Yahweh elohim* alone is God was essential to Israel's identity as God's covenant people.

Then as now, having no other gods besides the Lord is characterized by total commitment to the one and only God. "The first of the commandments, in sum, is the essential foundation for the building of the covenant community. Yahweh had opened himself to a special relationship with Israel, but that relationship could develop only if Israel committed themselves to Yahweh alone. Yahweh had rescued them and freed them, delivered them and guided them, then dwelt with them. The next step, if there was to be a next step, belonged to them. If they were to remain in his Presence, they were not to have other gods."[7] The same is true of us today – if we are to remain in God's presence, we may not have other gods.

## For Discussion

1. Assuming that we worship other gods for a reason, what advantages do we think these other, lesser gods provide us?

2. What are some of the things we put "before God's face?" How can we keep these false gods from separating us from God?

3. How do we properly respond, as individuals and congregations, to the words that have been spoken by the God who has redeemed us?

4. What impact does the failure to worship and serve only the one true God have on the purity of the church; on the unity of the church?

## For reflection and response

What are some concrete steps we can take to make sure that we, our families, and our congregations successfully resist the ever-present temptations to worship other gods?

Pray and give God thanks for being the one true God. You may wish to pray Psalm 97, or to use that psalm as a model for your prayer.

## Additional Resources

*A Commentary on the Book of Exodus*, U. Cassuto (Jerusalem: The Magnes Press, 1967).

   Although not widely known, this commentary combines solid evangelical scholarship with a wealth of spiritual insight.

*Idols for Destruction: Christian Faith and its Confrontation with American Society*, Herbert Schlossberg (Nashville: Thomas Nelson, 1983).

   A powerful exploration of current cultural idols (including history, humanity, mammon, nature, power, and religion) that threaten to come between Christians and God.

# Endnotes

1. Bruce K. Waltke, *"dabar"* in *Theological Wordbook of the Old Testament* (Chicago: Moody Press, 1980), vol. I, p. 180.
2. Jack B. Scott, *"elohim"* in *Theological Wordbook of the Old Testament* (Chicago: Moody Press, 1980), vol. I, p. 93.
3. U. Cassuto, *A Commentary on the Book of Exodus* (Jerusalem: The Magnes Press, 1967), p. 241.
4. Cassuto, *Exodus*, p. 239.
5. John I. Durham, *Exodus* (Waco: Word, 1987), p. 285.
6. John J. Davis, *Moses and the Gods of Egypt: Studies in Exodus* (Grand Rapids: Baker, 1986), p. 210.
7. Durham, *Exodus*, p. 285.

# O Lᴏʀᴅ, Our Lord

Nature is too thin a screen;
the glory of the omnipresent God burst through everywhere.
*Ralph Waldo Emerson*

## Overview

Psalm 8 poetically and prayerfully expresses the basic teachings of Genesis 1-2: God created the entire universe and is therefore the rightful ruler over all creation. When God created man and woman, he specifically charged them with the responsibility of overseeing his earthly creation. This psalm encourages us to regain both a fuller understanding of the sovereignty of God and a biblically rooted appreciation of our responsibility to be faithful stewards of God's good creation.

---

### Read: Psalm 8:1-9

### For Discussion

1. *Who are the people to whom you owe obedience? Who are those required to do as you say?*

2. *What can we learn from these verses about God as our Lord and the Lord of all creation?*

# The Text

## *Psalm 8:1-9*

### *O LORD [YHWH], our Lord [adonai] (v. 1)*

At the outset of this psalm, God is first addressed as Yahweh (see Lesson 3), then as *adonai*, from a Hebrew root meaning "lord."

The singular *adon* is found throughout the Old Testament. It is used to indicate a master of slaves (Gen. 24:14) and the ruler of subjects (Gen. 45:8). It is also used by Sarah to refer to Abraham (Gen. 18:12), by Lot in addressing the angelic visitors (Gen. 19:2), by Hannah when addressing Eli (I Sam. 1:15), and by Saul's servants when addressing Saul (I Sam. 16:16).

However, the special plural form *adonai* refers exclusively to God. It occurs more than 300 times in the Old Testament, mostly in the Psalms and prophetic books. "Just as *elohim* (God) is plural in the Hebrew [see Lesson 4], so this word might also be called an intensive plural or plural of majesty."[1]

In later Judaism, *adonai* took on additional significance. Devout Jews, fearful that the inadvertent mispronunciation of *YHWH* would violate the commandment against taking the Lord's name in vain, began to use *adonai* as a substitute. When they came to the word *YHWH* in their public reading of Scripture, they would say *adonai*, in much the same way that we would say "that is" instead of simply reading the abbreviation "i.e."

The reference to Yahweh as *our* Lord is very pointed. Yahweh is not merely the psalmist's personal deity, but the God of the people of Israel. And it is Yahweh, not any other god or gods, who is the God of Israel and the psalmist.

### *what is man that you are mindful of him (v. 4)*

"From an objective perspective, human beings are but the tiniest fragments in a giant universe; it is not conceivable that they could have significance or a central position. But the name of God, through which revelation comes, indicates that the very opposite is true."[2]

In contrast to God, the heavens are indeed tiny, having been pushed and prodded into shape by the divine digits; yet in contrast to the heavens, with its millions of galaxies spread out over billions of light years of space, the human race seems appallingly inconsequential. So it is easily understandable that we, like the psalmist, may find ourselves gazing at the glories of the nighttime sky and asking God "what is man?"[3]

## *You made him ruler over the works of your hands (v. 6)*

Despite our sense of smallness and insignificance, God has a very special role for his human creation: We are charged to rule over the works of his hands.

The Hebrew word for "rule," *mashal*, illustrates "the importance of the principle of authority, the absolute moral necessity of respect for proper authority, the value of it for orderly society and happy living and the origin of all authority in God."[4]

God, the Creator, as ultimate Lord, has delegated responsibility to his human creation. Our rule requires our continuous, faithful response to the creator who entrusted us with this enormous responsibility. And to learn about our responsibilities we must first and foremost devote ourselves to the study, not of nature, but of nature's God.

"The person who reflects upon nature ... will certainly be impressed, but the impression will not imprint any truth in the mind with respect to mankind's role in the universe. In fact, the opposite is the case; the honest person's gaze into the vastness of space evokes only a sense of smallness." That is because "the role of human beings in the universe, in other words, is not something which can be discerned from reflecting upon nature, or from a kind of natural philosophy; it is something which may be known only on the basis of special and specific revelation."[5]

*O Lord, our Lord, how majestic is your name in all the earth! (v. 9)*

It is noteworthy that in this psalm, which sings about the role of men and women in God's creation, *God* has been the subject of most of the verbs. That Psalm 8 ends where it began, praising the majesty of the divine name, helps us understand its central meaning.

God's "name" represents not only God, but also God's self-revelation. God's name and God's majesty are poetically synonymous, for the majesty of both God's person and creation are revealed in the divine name and all that it implies. The majestic name of God both permeates the earth and transcends the heavens, thus evoking words of praise. For it was the revelation of the name that transformed humanity's sense of its own insignificance into an awareness of God's plan for his chosen people.

## For Discussion

1. What does the simultaneous consideration of our tininess in the cosmos and our enormous value in God's eyes say to us?

2. Have you ever delegated authority over something very special to someone else? What enabled you to give another that responsibility? In doing so, were you taking any risks?

3. What do we learn about the character of God from the fact that he has given his human creation authority to rule over the works of his hands? How have we used, and misused, that authority?

4. What do God's nature and activities teach us about the proper exercise of our own authority?

# The Teachings

Two key teachings that emerge from this psalm are God's lordship over all creation and human stewardship as we rule over the works of God's hands.

## God's lordship

As we saw above, one name by which God has revealed himself is "lord," (*adonai* in Hebrew, *kyrios* in Greek). The earliest Christians transferred that "name" to the risen Jesus. Thomas' great confession "My Lord [*kyrios*] and my God" (John 20:28) is one notable example. And in a particularly poetic passage Paul wrote that "God exalted [Jesus] to the highest place and gave him the name that is above every name, that at the name of Jesus every knee should bow, in heaven and on earth and under the earth, and every tongue confess that Jesus Christ is Lord [*kyrios*], to the glory of God the Father" (Phil. 2:9-11).

These confessions are not simply intellectual assertions that Jesus Christ is fully God. They are personal affirmations that Jesus is Lord. Lordship is always personal, for "In the concept of the lord two things are conjoined in organic unity: the exercise of power as such and the personal nature of its exercise."[6]

In the Roman empire, the phrase, *Kyrios Kaiser*, "Caesar is Lord," was used to acknowledge the deity of the emperor. It was also used as a loyalty oath. Christians who affirmed that Jesus, not Caesar, was God were put to death. In this century, the Barmen Declaration, written in Germany by Christians struggling under Adolph Hitler's dictatorship, was a courageous affirmation that no human political leader could demand the absolute obedience due God alone.

Even now the historic Christian teaching that God is Lord is not terribly popular. In some circles, the very word "lord" is deemed inseparable from "patriarchal oppression." For a culture that has nearly deified the notion of individual liberty, the idea of offering unqualified allegiance to another, even God, cuts too hard against the modern trend toward absolute autonomy. Even in the Church some prefer to label God Facilitator and Friend, a cosmic companion who is only to be enjoyed but not obeyed. What is lost in such inadequate characterizations is God's self-revelation as Lord, the one who is sovereign over all creation, the one who requires from us a personal response of worshipful service and rightful obedience.

## *Human stewardship*

To correctly understand that God is lord of all creation is to begin to recognize that God's lordship affects every aspect of our lives, particularly our stewardship of God's creation. It is to realize that humanity is not alone in the cosmos. An incomplete or inaccurate understanding of God as Lord over all creation can lead to distorted views not only of the nature of our stewardship but of the nature of creation itself.

As Tony Campolo observes, "There really *is* a tendency for many Christians, who become 'green' in their activism and commit themselves to making environmental issues a vital part of their faith, to also become seriously confused in their thinking. ... there really is some truth to the accusation that some green Christians end up talking very much like New Agers and in time end up espousing some New Age theology."[7]

One of the more persistent and pernicious New Age notions is that all nature – people, animals, trees, rocks – are equally divine. However, "Nature is not divine. It is the creation of God, not a god or goddess. When treated as divine, the superficially benign face of nature is revealed for what it is. Invariably, human sacrifice is demanded."[8]

If that assessment sounds extreme, consider the following remarks by Ingrid Newkirk, director of People for the Ethical Treatment of Animals, and Dave Foreman of Earth First! Says Newkirk, "Animal liberationists do not separate out the human animal, so there is no rational basis for saying that a human being has special

rights ... I don't believe that human beings have 'the right to life.'"
And in arguing against feeding people starving to death in Ethiopia,
Foreman asserted that "The worst thing we could do in Ethiopia is to
give aid – the best thing would be to just let nature seek its own bal-
ance, to let the people there just starve."[9]

It is a profound misunderstanding of the Christian view of creation to teach that animals and plants have the same "rights" as
humans, that a person made in the image of God is of no more value
to God than a tree. "Are not two sparrows sold for a penny? Yet not
one of them will fall to the ground apart from the will of your Father.
And even the very hairs of your head are all numbered. So don't be
afraid; you are worth more than many sparrows." (Matt. 10:29-31)
And God clearly approves of eating fruit (Gen. 2:9, 16) and meat
(Gen. 9:1-3; Acts 10:10-15).

The best way to avoid becoming "seriously confused" in our
thinking about our stewardship of creation is to study carefully what
Scripture teaches about God as Lord, and about our responsibilities
to the Lord who has charged us to rule over creation. Only if we
acknowledge that there is a God who made heaven and earth, a God
in whose image we have been made, a God who has given us the
responsibility of ruling over the works of his hands, can we have a
biblically balanced view of our stewardship of creation.

## For Discussion

1. What are our responsibilities in ruling over the works of
God's hands? What are some practical ways in which we can
fulfill our responsibilities?

2. How does the biblical teaching about creation differ from
New Age conceptions about life on earth?

3. Describe a proper, healthy, biblical view of human stewardship of God's creation.

# The Life of the Church

The idea of submitting to God as "lord" is not terribly popular today. And one of the most obvious results of denying God's sovereignty is seen in the damage that has been done to the earth. While some blame Christian doctrines for the current "ecological crisis," Elizabeth Achtemeier understands that "Far from being the source of our ecological crisis, the biblical understanding of our dominion over the earth, as stewards of God's land and servants of his will, should act as a powerful check on all of our proud attempts to claim that we can do with the natural world as we will. No, we cannot. 'The earth is the Lord's and the fulness thereof,' and we are always responsible to him."

She continues, "In short, pollution takes place when God is ignored and when we no longer believe ourselves responsible to him. Then we become our own gods and goddesses, or we manufacture our own idols, and the world becomes the place where our will rules supreme and we can do with the creation and other human beings anything we like."[10]

In Psalm 8, the psalmist looks to humanity's nature, position, and destiny in the original purpose of God. Similarly, the prophets and apostles look forward to the destined restoration of humanity's relation to God and to creation (See Isa. 11:1-9; Rom. 8:18-22). As we recover a biblical understanding of God as our Lord, and of God as Lord of all creation, we are properly able to worship and serve God alone, and to rule faithfully over the works of his hands.

---

### *For Discussion*

1. What does it mean for us to call God "Lord?" In what areas of life is it particularly difficult to yield to God's lordship?

2. What are some of the practical ways in which our lives demonstrate God's lordship?

## *For reflection and response*

What specific actions can we as individuals, families, and congregations take to recognize God as our Lord in all areas of life, specifically in our stewardship of creation?

Pray and give God thanks that he alone is Lord of all the universe. You may wish to pray Psalm 135:1-7, or to use those verses as a model for your prayer.

## Additional Resources

*Nature, God & Pulpit*, Elizabeth Achtemeier (Grand Rapids: Eerdmans, 1992).

Essays and sermons designed to provide preachers with resources concerning "the biblical materials having to do with the natural world and God's relation to it."

*How to Rescue the Earth Without Worshiping Nature: A Christian's Call to Save Creation*, Tony Campolo (Nashville: Nelson, 1992).

A popular, readable, and very informative attempt to remind modern Christians that God, not his creation, is the only proper object of our worship.

*The Cross and the Rain Forest: A Critique of Radical Green Spirituality*, Robert Whelan, Joseph Kirwan, Paul Haffner (Grand Rapids: Eerdmans/ Acton Institute, 1996).

A thoroughly documented critique of "secular environmentalist ideology" and its divergences from historic Christian teachings about God and creation.

## Endnotes

1. Robert L. Alden *"adon"* in *Theological Wordbook of the Old Testament* (Chicago: Moody Press, 1980) vol I, p. 13.
2. Peter C. Craigie, *Psalms 1-50* (Waco: Word, 1983), p. 108.
3. A note about various Bible translations: Some contemporary translations of Scripture, in an attempt to be "inclusive," intentionally mistranslate verses such as these, replacing the singular with the plural. For example, the New Revised Standard Version translates this verse, "what are

human beings that you are mindful of them, mortals that you care for them?" The loss of the collective singular "man," meaning human not male, robs this verse of much of its poetry and power and diminishes the accuracy of the translation.

4. Victor P. Hamilton, *"mashal"* in *Theological Wordbook of the Old Testament* (Chicago: Moody Press, 1980) vol. I, p. 534.

5. Craigie, *Psalms*, p. 109.

6. Werner Foerster, *"kyrios"* in *Theological Dictionary of the New Testament* (Grand Rapids: Eerdmans, 1965), vol. 3, p. 1040.

7. Tony Campolo, *How to Rescue the Earth Without Worshiping Nature: A Christian's Call to Save Creation* (Nashville: Nelson, 1992), p. 4.

8. John K. Williams, "Gary Cooper, Humane Existence and Deep Ecology," in *Religion & Liberty* (Autumn, 1992), p. 15.

9. Cited in Robert Whelan, Joseph Kirwan, and Paul Haffner, *The Cross and the Rain Forest: A Critique of Radical Green Spirituality* (Grand Rapids: Eerdmans/The Acton Institute, 1996), p. 75.

10. Elizabeth Achtemeier, *Nature, God & Pulpit* (Grand Rapids: Eerdmans, 1992) pp. 67-68.

# The All-Sufficient God

Let us bring what is our own, God will supply the rest.
*John Chrysostom*

## Overview

In the opening verses of Genesis 17, God reveals himself to Abram as *el-shaddai*, reaffirms his covenant with Abram, and changes Abram's name to Abraham. Through these acts, God provides us with important information about his own nature and about the nature of his covenant relationship with his people. In these revelations we find a source of strength and courage for living faithful lives in difficult times.

---

### Read: Genesis 17:1-5

### For Discussion

*1. How do our agreements with other people, formal and informal, influence or determine our interactions with them?*

*2. What do we learn from these verses about God's nature and the nature of God's relationship with Abram?*

# The Text

## Genesis 17:1-5

Twenty-four years after having promised Abram, "I will make of you a great nation" (Gen. 12:1-9), God here reveals himself as "God Almighty," *el-shaddai.*

### I am God Almighty [el-shaddai] (v. 1)

As we saw in Lesson 3, until God revealed himself to Moses as *YHWH,* he was known by his name *el-shaddai. El* is the Hebrew equivalent of the English word "god." It can be translated with a lower case "g" to indicate a deity, or with a capital "G" to identify or address the God of Abraham. *El* conveys a sense of might and power, as in Psalm 77:14, "You are the God [*el*] who performs miracles; you display your power among the peoples."

The derivation of *shaddai* is less certain. The traditional translation, "Almighty," goes back to early Jewish rabbis, who understood the word to mean "self-sufficient." Other Old Testament scholars trace *shaddai* to a Hebrew root meaning "strong," "powerful," or "violent." *El-shaddai* is thus the God who reveals himself by special deeds of power. This was the understanding of the Greek translation of the Old Testament, which uses *pantokrator,* "all-powerful," and of Jerome, whose use of *omnipotens* in his fourth-century translation of the Bible into Latin has influenced English translations of Scripture from the King James Version to the present.

Some more recent interpreters suggest that *shaddai* may be derived from the Hebrew word for "breast." They propose the translation "the all-sufficient God," that is, the God who gives life, the God who sustains life, the God who blesses, nourishes, nurtures, and comforts. Certainly this is the sense conveyed by *shaddai* in the blessing given by Jacob, Abraham's grandson, to his own son Joseph,

"Joseph is a fruitful vine, a fruitful vine near a spring ... because of your father's God [*el*] who helps you, because of the Almighty [*shaddai*] who blesses you with the blessings of the heavens above, blessings of the deep that lies below, blessings of the breast and womb" (Gen. 49:22, 25). Isaiah uses similar imagery, as when he writes of God giving birth to and nursing his people until they "delight in [God's] overflowing abundance" (Isa. 66:11).

## walk before me and be blameless (v. 1)

God revealed his name to Abram before he told Abram to walk before him and be blameless. The sequence is significant. God did not come to Abram and say "If you walk before me and are blameless, then and only then will I reveal to you my name." Rather, Abram's blameless walk before God was to be his response to God's gracious self-revelation.

The word translated "blameless" comes from a root that conveys the idea of completeness. It does not mandate a precondition that must be met before God will fulfill his part of the covenant, but points to a relationship with God characterized by the absolute, unqualified surrender of our will to the will of God. Here given to Abram, this same command would later be given to the whole people of Israel (Deut. 18:13).

## I will confirm my covenant between me and you (v. 2)

A covenant clarifies the relationship between two parties without requiring that those parties be equal. It transforms an uncertain, therefore potentially troublesome, situation into a supportive community by means of binding regulations.

A biblical covenant may be defined as "an unchangeable, divinely imposed legal agreement between God and man that stipulates the conditions of their relationship."[1] Since God is the author of the covenant, it is not our human prerogative to alter its terms. Once we have agreed to the terms of God's covenant, that is, once we have accepted the salvation he offers us, our responsibility is to live a life that honors the privileges and the obligations of our covenant relationship with God.

As God progressively revealed his nature through revealing his names, so God's successive covenants with his people teach us more and more about how he intends for us to relate to him. In his covenant with Noah "and every living creature," God promised never again to destroy all life on earth by a flood (Gen. 9:12-16). In his covenant with Abraham he promised to establish his chosen people (Gen. 17:9-11). In his covenant with the people of Israel God spelled out in great detail his expectations for his people (Ex. 19-24). These covenants all point to the new covenant God now has with his people, which was made possible by the life, death, and resurrection of Jesus Christ (Luke 22:20, I Cor. 11:25).

### *Abram fell face down (v. 3)*

In response to God's revelation of his name and reaffirmation of his covenant, Abram fell on his face. In contrast to those who would reduce God to an impersonal force, a projection of human personality, or the sum of the whole universe, Abram recognizes, and is overwhelmed by, the very real presence of the One who transcends human imagination and experience. Abram's faithful response reminds us that it is a truly awesome thing to find oneself in the presence of Almighty God.

### *your name will be Abraham (v. 5)*

As he reaffirmed his intention to supply all he had promised, God also changed Abram's name from "exalted father" to Abraham, "father of a multitude." This change of name marks an important turn in Abram's life. In a similar way, God will later announce a new dimension to his relationship with Abraham's descendants when, as part of his call to lead the Israelites out of slavery in Egypt, he tells Moses, "I am the LORD. I appeared to Abraham, to Isaac and to

Jacob as God Almighty [*el-shaddai*], but by my name the L ORD [*YHWH*] I did not make myself known to them" (Ex. 6:2-3).

## *For Discussion*

1. What other passages of Scripture come to mind as you consider the all-sufficiency of God?

2. What is the significance of Abram's new name? What do you make of the fact that he got this new name before the promise was fulfilled?

3. What do these verses have to offer "seekers," those with a vague but unsatisfied spiritual longing?

# The Teachings

Two key teachings that emerge from these verses are God's ability and willingness to supply all our needs and the nature of God's covenant with us.

## *The All-Sufficient God*

To Abram – who at God's calling left a settled homeland, comfortable circumstances, family, and friends to go on a long, possibly dangerous journey to a place he did not know – God promised land, an incalculable number of descendants, and a spiritual mission.

Abram had lived three quarters of a century when those promises first were made, and he waited nearly a quarter-century more for their fulfillment. It was in his own good time that the all-sufficient God, the God who nurtures and makes fruitful, fulfilled the promise he had made decades before. Abraham learned that what God promises, only God can deliver. He learned that, in and of himself, he was not sufficient. He learned that God alone is *el-shaddai*.

Such knowledge of God contrasts sharply with those modern spiritualities termed "New Age." The New Age movement tends to view individuals as utterly autonomous, completely self-sufficient, and even divine. Whatever we need, New Age enthusiasts suggest, we can find within ourselves. As Jack Underhill, publisher of *Life Times Magazine* boldly declares, "YOU are the only thing that is real," and even "You are God."[2]

Against this trend we modern Christians need to recognize and admit our own limitations. We need to accept that we are finite creatures. Only if we admit that we are not divine, only if we realize that our own resources are insufficient to meet our needs, only then can we begin to experience the all-sufficiency of God. As Nathan Stone writes:

"To experience God's fullness one must empty self. It is not easy to empty self. It was never easy to do that. The less empty of self we are, the less of blessing God can pour into us; the more of pride and self-sufficience, the less fruit we can bear. ... As the all-sufficient One he says, 'Apart from me you can do nothing.'"[3]

## The covenant of God

"The God of Israel stands before us as one God – invisible, Creator of all things, ruler of nature and history – absolutely unique in the ancient world. But that is not all. Israel did not believe merely that such a God existed; she was convinced that this God had, in a historical act, chosen her, entered into covenant with her, and made her his people."[4]

The history of God's chosen people is marked by swings between attempts to fulfill their covenant responsibilities and their rejection of that bond in favor of dalliances with other deities. Nor have Christians ever completely overcome the temptation to be unfaithful to our all-sufficient God. Specifically, Christian history has been plagued by "antinomianism," the mistaken belief that God's unconditional grace frees us from our covenant obligation to live according to God's revelation.

Gabriel Fackre defines a covenant as "the solemn promise to fulfill a declared purpose." He notes that, "Covenant has to do with the divine promise to keep the divine purpose ... Covenant in the biblical perspective is the stubborn, unswerving commitment to the Shalom [peace] God wills for the world. But more than a general faithfulness to the purpose, it is a pledge to execute this intention through a particular people."[5]

Repeated biblical references to "covenant" are reassuring reminders that God has chosen us to be his people. They also remind us that just as there are blessings in upholding the covenant, so there are curses that come as a consequence of its willful violation: "Be careful to follow every command I am giving you today, so that you may live and increase and may enter and possess the land that the LORD promised on oath to your forefathers. ... If you ever forget the LORD your God and follow other gods and worship and bow down to them, I testify against you today that you will surely be destroyed" (Deut. 8:1, 19).

As Fackre observes, "Covenant is a demand as well as a gift. ... While no human act of obedience or disobedience can make or break the covenant, judgment attends our disdain of it and faithlessness to it. ... imperatives do keep company with the indicatives of election."[6]

## For Discussion

1. In what ways has God shown you that he is sufficient to meet your needs?

2. What types of human "covenants" are similar to the covenant God established with Abram?

3. What is the message for us in the reality that God's faithfulness, not ours, keeps the covenant bond secure?

4. What difference does it make to know that our God can supply all our needs?

# The Life of the Church

In Abram's day, some 1,800 years before the birth of Christ, most people believed the world was ruled by unknown divine forces – good and evil spirits that had to be discovered and appeased, lest by inadvertent inattention helpless humans anger capricious deities into causing sickness, famine, or flood.

This was the context in which God revealed himself to Abram as *el-shaddai*.

It is all too easy for modern Christians to overlook the dramatic and decisive nature of this self-revelation. Once God revealed his name to Abram, and established a covenant with him, Abram, and through him all people, no longer had to fear giving accidental offense to unknown deities or arbitrary cosmic powers. Now all people could freely worship and serve the God who made himself known as the One who alone can, and indeed desires to, supply all human needs.

Not only did God reveal himself by name, but in establishing his covenant with Abram God also obligated himself to fulfill certain responsibilities. In so doing, God listed the duties of those who entered into this covenant relationship with him. God's covenant with his people is not, as some suppose, a whimsical list of "thou-shalt-nots" created by a cosmic killjoy to keep people from having a good time. Rather, this covenant is the gift of *el-shaddai*, the all-sufficient God. The responsibilities God requires of us are intended for our benefit. They are an expression of unmerited favor, which enable us to enjoy God, and God's creation, to the fullest.

God's covenant is itself an act of self-revelation. As John H. Walton writes, "God has a plan in history that he is sovereignly executing. The goal of that plan is for him to be in relationship with the people whom he has created. It would be difficult for people to enter into a relationship with a God whom they do not know. If his nature were concealed, obscured, or distorted, an honest relationship would be impossible." God wants people to know him. "The purpose of the covenant is to reveal God."[7]

New Age ideologies are simply revivals of ancient pagan beliefs that human life is surrounded by cosmic forces that must be appeased. Christians can, and must, respond to such ideologies by acknowledging and proclaiming God's self-revelation as *el-shaddai*. For in announcing his name to Abram, and in establishing his covenant with him, God has revealed himself to be the One who alone is able to supply every human need, above all the inescapable human need to be in a personal relationship with God.

## For Discussion

1. How is God's covenant an act of God's self-revelation?
2. How well does the word "covenant" characterize your personal relationship with God?
3. What difference can the covenant faithfulness of God make in our devotional life? Our worship? Our mission?

## For reflection and response

Knowing that God alone is fully able to supply all human needs, what responsibilities do Christians have to make God's all-sufficiency known to a desperately needy world? What are some ways in which we can fulfill these responsibilities?

Pray and give God thanks that he is able and willing to supply all our needs. You may wish to pray Psalm 67, or to use that psalm as a model for your prayer.

## Additional Resources

*Understanding the New Age*, Russell Chandler (Grand Rapids: Zondervan, 1993).
Explores the many facets of the New Age movement and offers responses grounded in Scripture and historic Christian teachings.

*Spirit Wars: Pagan Revival in Christian America*, Peter Jones (Mukilteo, Wash.: Winepress Publishing and Escondido, Calif.: Main Entry Editions, 1997).

This carefully documented work traces many of the "spirits" of the modern age back to their roots in ancient pagan spiritualities.

*Covenant: God's Purpose, God's Plan*, John H. Walton (Grand Rapids: Zondervan, 1994).

Starting from the fact that God desires to make himself known in order to be in relationship with human beings, Walton describes the biblical covenant as the "mechanism that drives" God's self-revelation.

## Endnotes

1. Wayne Grudem, *Systematic Theology* (Grand Rapids: Zondervan, 1994), p. 515.
2. Cited in Russell Chandler, *Understanding the New Age* (Grand Rapids: Zondervan, 1993), pp. 28-29.
3. Nathan J. Stone, *Names of God* (Chicago: Moody Press, 1944), p. 49.
4. John Bright, *The Kingdom of God: The Biblical Concept and Its Meaning For the Church* (New York: Abingdon Press, 1953), p. 26.
5. Gabriel Fackre, *The Christian Story: A Narrative Interpretation of Basic Christian Doctrine* (Grand Rapids: Eerdmans, 1984), pp. 89-90.
6. Fackre, *The Christian Story*, p. 90.
7. John H. Walton, *Covenant: God's Purpose, God's Plan* (Grand Rapids: Zondervan, 1994), p 24.

# Honoring the Father

God is not just any God, capable of being named according to human
fancy. No, God is the one whom Jesus reveals as his Father.

*Elizabeth Achtemeier*

## Overview

Jesus called God *abba*, Father. When he did, his claim of intimacy angered certain Jewish religious leaders. For different reasons,
some today take offense when God's children address God as
"Father." To reject Jesus' example of calling God "Father" is to
impoverish both the Church and the world. To claim this great privilege is to enrich our personal and corporate relationship with God.
As we study Jesus' use of *abba* in talking to, and about, God the
Father we gain irreplaceable insights into the nature of God and the
nature of human fatherhood.

---

### Read: John 5:16-23

### For Discussion

*1. What might cause people today to shy away from calling
God "Father?"*

*2. What do Jesus' words to the religious leaders who chal-
lenged him reveal about the nature of God and God's work in
the world?*

# The Text

## *John 5:16-23*

At the outset of John 5, Jesus heals a man who had been ill for 38 years, commanding him to "Get up! Pick up your mat and walk." That Jesus healed on the Sabbath angered certain Jews. That he called God "Father" angered them even more.

### *Jesus said to them, "My Father ..." (v. 17)*

In their corporate worship, the Jews of Jesus' day occasionally referred to God as "our Father." But God is called "Father" only 15 times in the Old Testament, and in every instance God is spoken of as the Father of the nation of Israel, never as the Father of an individual Israelite. The very personal way in which Jesus addressed God as "*my* Father" unequivocally identified the unique Father-Son relationship Jesus claimed to have with the God of Abraham, Isaac, and Jacob. In the gospels Jesus speaks of, or to, God as his Father 170 times.

The Aramaic word underlying our English "Father," is *abba*. *Abba*, which might also be translated "Daddy," is a term of endearment less formal than "Father." *Abba* is a form of address that could be freely used by toddlers yet used without embarrassment by adult children as well. The personal nature of this term is shown by the fact that slaves were not permitted to use *abba* when addressing the head of a family.[1]

### *For this reason the Jews tried all the harder to kill him (v. 18)*

The Jews perceived Jesus' healing on the Sabbath as a serious infraction, but, "*a man making himself equal with God* was quite rightly understood as challenging their fundamental distinction between the holy, infinite God and finite, fallen human beings. Various first-century pagan religions were quite happy to obliterate distinctions between God and humankind. If the exile had convinced the Jews of anything, it was that idolatry was always wrong and that God was wholly Other."[2] In the opinion of these Jews, Jesus had committed blasphemy.

In effect, Jesus was being charged with a rebellion similar to Adam and Eve's sinful attempt to be like God (see Gen. 3:5-6). What Jesus' accusers failed to recognize was that Jesus did not claim equality with God as another, competing God, but as God Incarnate, the Second Person of the Trinity.[3] Blinded by their preconceptions, most notably that God could not come to earth in human flesh, these religious leaders tried to destroy one whom they could not squeeze into their mold. God was revealing himself in human flesh, and their response was murderous rage.

It remains for us to grasp the divinely revealed truth that Jesus Christ *is* fully God as well as fully human. Unfortunately, even among modern church leaders there are those whose biases lead them to deny the Incarnation by reducing Jesus Christ to a good teacher or an excellent example of some sort of vague "God-consciousness." Such unbiblical understandings diminish God's triune nature and deny God's redemptive act in sending his only Son as the atonement for our sins. Now as then, the sad truth is that there have been times that Jesus "came to that which was his own, but his own did not receive him" (John 1:11).

## *For the Father loves the Son and shows him all he does (v. 20)*

The Son is able to do whatever the Father does because the Father loves the Son and continually shows him all that he is doing. The Son's love for the Father is displayed in the perfect obedience that finally leads him to the cross. By his obedience, Jesus is continually revealing the Father – doing the Father's deeds and carrying out the Father's will.

"This marvelous disclosure of the nature and character of God utterly depends, in the first instance, not on God's love of us, but on the love of the Father for the Son and in the love of the Son for the Father. ... The very obedience and dependence that characterize Jesus' utter subordination to the Father are themselves so perfect that all Jesus does is what the Father wills and does, so it is nothing less than the revelation of God. Small wonder that Jesus will later declare, 'Anyone who has seen me has seen the Father.'"[4]

### He who does not honor the Son does not honor the Father, who sent him (v. 23)

As we have seen, the Jews who criticized Jesus for healing on the Sabbath were enraged by his claim to be the very Son of God. Therefore it should come as no surprise that they were further shocked by his declaration that the Son is one with the Father not only in activity but also in honor. As C.S. Lewis has written, "You must make your choice. Either this man was, and is, the Son of God: or else a madman or something worse. You can shut Him up for a fool, you can spit at Him and kill Him as a demon; or you can fall at His feet and call him Lord and God."[5]

---

### For Discussion

1. If you were privileged to have a loving father, what is the most loving thing you remember your father doing for you? As you have aged, have you become more like your father in any way?

2. Try to put yourself in the position of a faithful Jew in first-century Palestine. How might you have felt about and responded to Jesus' assertion that God was his Father?

3. What does Jesus' reference to God as "*my* Father" reveal about the nature of Jesus' relationship with God? What does it reveal about our relationship with God?

4. What contributions do these verses make to discussions about the propriety of Christians calling God "Father?"

# The Teachings

Two key teachings that emerge from these verses are the Christian's privilege of calling God "Our Father" and the dangers of rejecting God as Father.

## *Calling God our Father*

"It is not self-evident to call God Father, as Jesus did. ... [I]n the Christian language about God, 'Father' is not an exchangeable metaphor, though otherwise it may be regarded as a metaphorical expression on the same footing with words like 'mother' or 'friend.' ... It was the only name for God Jesus used. ... Therefore, the exchange of this name inevitably results in turning to another God."[6]

In John 5:19-23 Jesus answers the Jewish objections to his healing on the Sabbath by specifically and insistently referring to God as his Father and to himself as God's Son. For the Jews of Jesus' day, who would not even pronounce the name of God (see Lesson 3), such references were nothing less than blasphemy. But for Jesus, this Father-Son relationship was at the heart of his earthly life and ministry.

That means that not only are these verses important for our understanding of the deity of Christ, they are also essential to our understanding of the Fatherhood of God.

## *Rejecting God as Father*

Attempts have been made in some segments of the church to exclude from Christian worship and service all references to God as "Father." Some endeavors are extreme examples of oversimplification, such as Mary Daly's aphorism, "If God is male then the male is God." Although cleverly phrased and widely quoted, this argument is easily refuted: No orthodox Christian theologian has ever ascribed male gender to God, nor does historic Christianity teach that men (or women) are divine.

As Aida Besançon Spencer writes, "God is Father not because God is masculine. God is Father because 'father' in the ancient world was a helpful metaphor to communicate certain aspects of God's character. God is Spirit, neither male nor female. God has no form at all (as God clearly revealed to Moses in Deut. 4:15-16). Therefore many metaphors and similes, actions, and descriptive adjectives are needed to help us understand God."[7]

Other efforts to remove the biblical and creedal language of "God the Father" from Christian discourse are dangerous and deceptive because they contain bits of truth. One such argument is that Christians should never refer to God as "Father" because the word "Father" cannot convey the entire reality of the relationship between God and humankind. It is true that no single name (nor indeed the whole of human language) can encompass all of God. However, that a name by itself is insufficient does not mean that it must never be used. "All deities are invoked by names, even if that name is only the name *God*."[8]

Certainly the single name "Father," isolated from the rest of Scripture, does not reveal all that can be known about God. But then the Bible and the creeds of the Church nowhere claim that "Father" is the only name by which God is known. What Scripture teaches, and what the Church has (until quite recently) universally affirmed, is that one of the ways in which God has made himself known to us is as "Father," and that we, as God's children, have received the gift of calling upon God as Jesus did, as *abba*, Father.

Those who insist that Christians refrain from using the biblical, creedal language of God the Father deny themselves, and would deny us all, irreplaceable insight into the nature and character of God as God has chosen to reveal himself to us. Those who renounce the biblical teaching of God as Father – on the grounds that Father is a "patriarchal" effort to superimpose the male experience of fatherhood onto a God who is beyond all human understanding – get the reality of God as Father exactly backwards. Fatherhood is an aspect of God's nature that has been revealed to us, not an aspect of male experience that we have applied to God.

Moreover, "If 'Father' rightly denotes the God of Jesus, the intentional choice to evade this name suggests linguistically either that the object of worship is in fact different from the God normally worshiped by Christians or that the worshippers have rejected their status as sons and daughters of God."[9] (See Romans 8:15-16.)

## For Discussion

1. What are some of the reasons given for rejecting the biblical language of "God the Father?" What are some ways of respectfully yet faithfully addressing those concerns?

2. What are some possible results of Christians abandoning biblical language about God?

3. What are some benefits of exercising our privilege to call God Father?

4. How can the fatherhood of God as revealed in the New Testament help us to become better parents? To heal family wounds?

# The Life of the Church

Paul writes, "For this reason I kneel before the Father, from whom all fatherhood in heaven and on earth derives its name" (Eph. 3:14-15).

The direction of the attribution is essential: Paul kneels before God as his Father because it is *from God* that "all fatherhood in heaven and on earth derives its name."

Calling God "Father" is not a human attempt to make God in man's image, nor is the fatherhood of God a distorted human analogy. Rather, fatherhood is an innate, inherent, uncreated aspect of the nature of God. Consequently, to address God as "Father" is neither to engage in sexist rhetoric, nor is it to settle for a merely human linguistic construction. Instead it is addressing God using one of the names by which God has revealed himself to us, the name that Jesus taught us to use.

Certainly the relationship between Christ the Son and God the Father is unique. But it is not entirely dissimilar to the father-child relationship God maintains with each of us. Jesus called God *abba*, a term a toddler would use as we say "Daddy," but equally a word that an adult child could use freely, one that conveys the familiarity and intimacy that exists between a father and his children.

Jesus called God "Father," which offended certain Jews. Jesus taught his disciples to call God "our Father," and his disciples were persecuted as he was. So it should not be surprising that there are some today who choose to take offense at those who use the language of the Bible and say with the saints who have gone before us, "I believe in God the Father."

Whenever we address God as "Father" we declare, to one another and the world, that there is Someone who cares for every individual as an ideal father would and should. It is to say that there is a transcendent God who wants to have a Father-child relationship with every human being. It is to say that this Father so loved the whole world that he sent his only Son to live with us and within us; that whoever believes in him should not perish but have eternal life.

## For Discussion

1. Why is it important to realize that God's fatherhood constitutes an essential part of God's being rather than an aspect of human experience projected onto God?

2. What can we learn about human fatherhood from God's self-revelation as our Father?

3. How can a proper understanding of God as Father minister to the needs of those who have been hurt by their fathers?

## *For reflection and response*

Looking back over these five lessons, what have you learned about God from the names by which God has revealed himself? How does God's self-revelation as "Father" fit into what you know about God's being and activity?

Pray and give God thanks for being our perfect Father. You may wish to pray the Lord's Prayer (Matt. 6:9-13), or to use those verses as a model for your own prayer.

## Additional Resources

"Why God is not Mother," Elizabeth Achtemeier, *Christianity Today* (August 16, 1993, Vol. 37, No. 9, pp. 16-23).
An effective response to those who object to calling God "Father."

"Father-Ruler: The Meaning of the Metaphor 'Father' for God in the Bible," Aida Besançon Spencer, *Journal of the Evangelical Theological Society* (Vol. 39, No. 3, September 1996), pp. 433-442.
Examines the nature of metaphor, simile, and analogy as a way of understanding the appropriateness of calling God "Father."

## Endnotes

1. Herbert Lockyear, *All the Divine Names and Titles in the Bible* (Grand Rapids: Zondervan, 1975), p. 70.
2. D.A. Carson, *The Gospel According to John* (Grand Rapids: Eerdmans, 1991), p. 249.
3. The precise relationship between Jesus Christ and God the Father was the most divisive issue in the life of the early church. The first ecumenical council, meeting in Nicea in A.D. 325, affirmed that Jesus was of one substance (*homoousia*) with the Father. (For a history of this controversy and its relevance to modern Christians see Parker T. Williamson, *Standing Firm: Reclaiming Christian Faith in Times of Controversy* [Lenoir, N.C.: PLC Publications, 1996].) The Nicene Creed, used by Protestants, Roman Catholics, and the Eastern Orthodox, remains the most widely accepted articulation of the biblical teaching that Jesus Christ is simultaneously fully God and fully human.

4. Carson, *John*, p. 252.
5. C.S. Lewis, *Mere Christianity* (New York: Macmillan, 1943), p. 56.
6. Wolfhart Pannenberg, *An Introduction to Systematic Theology* (Grand Rapids: Eerdmans, 1991), pp . 31-32.
7. Aida Besançon Spencer, "Father-Ruler: The Meaning of the Metaphor 'Father' for God in the Bible," *Journal of the Evangelical Theological Society* (Vol. 39, No. 3, September 1996), p. 442.
8. Donald D. Hook and Alvin F. Kimel, Jr., "Calling God 'Father:' A Theolinguistic Analysis," *Faith and Philosophy* (Vol. 12, No. 2, April 1995), p. 216.
9. Ibid.

# God's Presence

God fills all places by giving existence to everything
occupying those places.

*Thomas Aquinas*

## Overview

With this lesson we begin a study of three of God's attributes: omnipresence, omnipotence, and omniscience. While the terms themselves are derived from Latin roots (rather than Hebrew or Greek), the concepts they express are central to what the Bible reveals about God's nature and his relationship with all creation. In this lesson we will look at what it means to say that God is always present everywhere. And we will see how this potentially abstract doctrine is in fact a concrete source of comfort and assurance.

*Read: II Chronicles 6:12-21 and Acts 17:24-28*

*For Discussion*

*1. Talk about a time when you have felt the need to be in more than one place at one time. Do you find comforting or confusing (or both) the idea that God is everywhere at every moment?*

*2. What can we learn from these passages about the presence of God?*

# The Texts

## *II Chronicles 6:12-21*

As he stood before the temple altar, in front of the whole assembly of Israel, Solomon prayed a prayer of dedication for the Jerusalem temple. In so doing, he also taught valuable lessons about prayer and the presence of God both to those assembled and to those who hear him now.

### *The heavens, even the highest heavens, cannot contain you (v. 18)*

The Hebrew grammar in the first part of this verse uses a construction intended to express that which is "superlative to an exceptional degree." In this way, without using a technical term like "omnipresent," Solomon conveys the concept of a God who transcends the limitations of the created order, a God so great that the whole heavens cannot confine him, a God who is always present everywhere.

This understanding is confirmed in Jesus' encounter with the Samaritan woman, recorded in John 4:4-26. When the woman raised the question of the right place to worship, as if God were present only at one single physical location, Jesus replied "God is spirit" (John 4:24). "Christ's point is that while man, being 'flesh,' can only be present in one place at a time, God, being 'spirit,' is not so limited. God is non-material, non-corporeal, and therefore non-localized."[1]

### *this temple … this place of which you said you would put your Name there (v. 20)*

The connection of God's "Name" with the Jerusalem temple reflects the ancient conviction that a name in itself has effective power. Thus for Yahweh to put his Name in the temple at Jerusalem meant not only that prayers made in that place would be effective, but also that Yahweh would there reveal his will in a special manner.

This insight enables us to appreciate how Solomon reconciled the universal presence of Yahweh with his understanding that God's presence was to be uniquely found at the temple.

## Acts 17:24-28

While in Athens, awaiting the arrival of Silas and Timothy, Paul "was greatly distressed to see that the city was full of idols." After debating Jews in the synagogue and philosophers on the street, he was invited to share his faith in the Areopagas, the Athenian court with jurisdiction over matters of religion, morals, and education. Having commended the sincerity of the Athenian search for a deity worthy of worship, Paul began telling them about the one true God.

### The God who made the world ... does not live in temples built by hands. (v. 24)

Here Paul begins to tell his hearers about the one true God; the God of Abraham, Isaac, and Jacob; the God and Father of the Lord Jesus Christ. Paul describes God as the creator of all that exists and the Lord of all the universe. He declares that the true God is not confined within idols, shrines, or sanctuaries built by human hands. Since even the massive temple in Jerusalem, faithfully and lovingly built for the worship of the one true God, could not contain God, how much less the many shrines that dotted the Athenian Acropolis.

### God ... is not far from each one of us. (v. 27)

Perhaps better translated "and yet being not far from each one of us," the Greek grammar of this phrase conveys an emphatic negative. Even though God cannot be confined within any human construction, God *is not* far away from any of his human creation. Indeed, God has arranged all creation in such a way that men and women may readily find him. (See Rom. 1:20.)

This same truth is expressed in the Old Testament: "What other nation is so great as to have their gods near them the way the LORD our God is near us whenever we pray to him?" (Deut. 4:7) and "The LORD is near to all who call on him, to all who call on him in truth" (Ps. 145:18).

The people of Athens, like all those to whom Paul preached, needed to turn from worshiping imaginary deities and idols of their own creation to the worship of the one true God. As a part of leading his hearers to a knowledge of God, Paul succinctly explained that while God can never be confined to a particular place, God is always near to all of us, wherever we are.

---

### *For Discussion*

1. What does it mean to say that the heavens cannot contain God?

2. What is the significance of places of worship if they are not places that contain God?

3. If God does not occupy any place, how can we say that he is not far from us?

4. What are some of the benefits of knowing that God is always near to us?

---

# The Teachings

These two passages are among those that support the historic Christian teaching that God is present everywhere at all times. They also help us distinguish the Christian doctrine of omnipresence from the concept of pantheism.

## *God's omnipresence*

Put in its simplest form, the doctrine of God's omnipresence affirms that there is no place where God is not.

However, since God is spirit (John 4:24) and not a material being, God does not occupy any physical location. Therefore, to understand the presence of God we must go beyond the limiting concept of "place." This truth was recognized by Solomon and Paul, who made it clear that God cannot be held within a structure built by humans, or even within the universe God has created. While theological and philosophical discussions of God's omnipresence can become very complex, a biblical study of the presence of God reveals:

1. *That God is in the universe, everywhere present at the same time.* "No atomic particle is so small that God is not fully present to it, and no galaxy so vast that God does not circumscribe it. No space is without the divine presence. God is in touch with every part of creation."[2] As the Psalmist writes "Where can I go from your Spirit? Where can I flee from your presence? If I go up to the heavens, you are there; if I make my bed in the depths, you are there. If I rise on the wings of the dawn, if I settle on the far side of the sea, even there your hand will guide me, your right hand will hold me fast" (Ps. 139:7-10).

2. *That the universe and all that it contains is in God.* The phrase, "For in him we live and move and have our being" (Acts 17:28) may be a quote from a Greek poet. Regardless of its source, Paul uses the statement to convey in a few simple words the profound truth that human beings do not exist apart from the presence of God. Without God's creating and sustaining presence and power, human life would not exist. Indeed, apart from God's presence the very universe would not exist.

3. *God is separate from the universe in which He dwells.* All material things exist in the presence of God, but God remains separate from them. God is able to manifest his presence, as in the Garden of Eden with Adam and Eve, in the pillar of fire leading Israel out of Egypt or, supremely, in Jesus, who was not part God but all God (see Phil. 2:6; I John 5:20). Yet, "It is not a piece of God is here and another parcel there, but God in His whole essence and perfections; in His wisdom to guide us, His power to protect and support

us, His mercy to pity us, His fullness to refresh us, and His goodness to relieve us: He is ready to sparkle out in this or that perfection, as the necessities of His people require, and His own wisdom directs for His own honor."[3]

Characteristics of God's omnipresence include God's being unlimited (Ps. 139:7), inescapable (Gen. 3:8), awesome (Jer. 5:22), directing (Ex. 13:21-22; Deut. 31:15), joyous (Ps. 16:11; Rom. 14:17), refreshing (Ex. 33:14; Isa. 40:31; Heb. 4:9), and visible (Ex. 33:9-10). As a result, God's omnipresence offers protection in times of crisis and difficulty (Isa. 43:1-2; Ps. 125:2); encourages us in prayer (Ps. 145:18; 73:28; Isa. 55:6; James 4:8); and, perhaps most important, gives our lives a sense of stability (Ps. 16:8; Deut. 33:27).[4]

## God's omnipresence distinguished from pantheism

God is always present to all material things, yet he remains separate from them. To claim the contrary, to say that God is the universe and the universe is God, is to reject Christianity and embrace pantheism.

Pantheism (from the Greek *pan* meaning "all" and *theos* meaning "God") may be defined as the belief that "God" is another word for the sum total of the contents of the universe. The term goes back to the eighteenth-century English author John Toland, a student of Hegel, who "thought of the deity as a divine organism inclusive of all lesser organisms. ... Toland coined the word *pantheism* and held that the universe is God."[5]

Some Eastern religions, such as Hinduism and Buddhism, incorporate an essentially pantheistic world view. Pantheism also underlies many so-called "New Age" beliefs. Physicist/philosopher Fritjof Capra exemplifies this school of thought when he writes that "all boundaries and dualisms have been transcended and all individuality dissolves into universal, undifferentiated oneness."[6] Pantheism, however, is ultimately irreconcilable with what Scripture reveals about the nature and the presence of God.

The biblical understanding of the nature of God is that the Creator is distinct from creation. The consistent witness of Scripture demonstrates that the Christian's faith in a God who is everywhere is utterly incompatible with the pantheistic belief that "God" is simply another name for the contents of the universe.

As Paul told the Athenians, "The God who made the world and everything in it is the Lord of heaven and earth  ... We are his offspring" (Acts 17:24, 28). Paul reminds us the right relationship between God and the world is that of Creator to creation, a teaching that clearly refutes any suggestion that Christian faith is compatible with pantheism.

This is also the message of the psalmist, "Praise the LORD from the earth, you great sea creatures and all ocean depths, lightning and hail, snow and clouds, stormy winds that do his bidding, you mountains and all hills, fruit trees and all cedars, wild animals and all cattle, small creatures and flying birds, kings of the earth and all nations, you princes and all rulers on earth, young men and maidens, old men and children" (Ps. 148:7-12).

Essential to our Christian understanding of the nature of God is that the Creator is distinct from creation. The consistent witness of Scripture demonstrates that the Christian's faith in a God who is everywhere is incompatible with the pantheistic belief that God is everything. And as we saw in Lesson 4, remaining aware of God's constant presence requires us to remove from our lives all competing "gods."

## For Discussion

1. How is our understanding of God as Creator (Lesson 1) linked to our understanding that God is present everywhere at all times?

2. What is the appeal of pantheism?

3. Why are pantheism and Christianity irreconcilable?

# The Life of the Church

We live in a world where it seems the only constant is change. Economic conditions often lead to frequent changes of jobs, careers, and locations; families are all too often torn apart by divorce, disease, and death; social institutions we once thought secure are succumbing to pressures from within and without; many of our communities have been reduced to isolated (and isolating) enclaves of scared and lonely individuals.

In a society that seems to have lost all sense of rootedness, the doctrine of God's omnipresence provides Christians with a firm foundation for stable personal, family, and professional lives. Although the term "omnipresence" may seem somewhat imposing, the historic Christian teaching that there is no place where God is not can be a continual source of comfort to all Christians. For the assurance that God is with us, through every change of employment, location, or family situation, is one way in which God provides each of us with "the peace of God, which transcends all understanding" (Phil. 4:7).

To be sure, the omnipresence of God must be understood in a spiritual, not material, sense (see Jer. 23:24; Isa. 66:1). As Brian Davies observes, "We cannot say that God is everywhere by virtue of being physically anywhere. But since places are part of creation, and since God is present to everything created as its Creator, then God can be said to be everywhere by being present to all places as their Creator."[7]

Because God transcends our finite human understandings of time and place, we can rest assured that wherever we are, there God is with us. Therefore, the doctrine of God's omnipotence "is more than a cold, abstract idea without personal significance to worshipers. It is an intimate comfort to supplicants to know of and experience the divine availability."[8]

### For Discussion

1. What would you say to a Christian who asked you to explain how it is possible for God to be everywhere at the same time? To a non-Christian?

2. In what specific ways can the historic Christian understanding of God's omnipresence support and encourage individual Christians and Christian congregations that might face unsettled or unsettling circumstances?

3. What is the significance of God's omnipresence for our daily Christian life?

### For reflection and response

When have you felt especially lonely? Did God's omnipresence bring you comfort and support in that situation? Consider that experience again in light of what you have learned from this study.

Pray and give God thanks that he is present everywhere at all times. You may want to pray Psalm 139, or to use that psalm as a model for your prayer.

## Additional Resources

*Thinking about God*, Brian Davies (London: Geoffrey Chapman, 1985).
Thoughtfully makes the case for the rationality of belief in God. Includes a helpful chapter on God's omnipresence, omniscience, and omnipotence.

*The Living God: Systematic Theology: Volume One,* Thomas C. Oden (San Francisco: HarperSanFrancisco, 1987)
Chapter 2, "The Nature of God," contains Oden's reflections on God's omnipresence, omnipotence, and omniscience as well as references to relevant Scripture passages and the writings of earlier theologians.

# Endnotes

1. J.I. Packer, *Knowing God* (Downers Grove: InterVarsity Press, 1973), p. 109.
2. Thomas C. Oden, *The Living God: Systematic Theology: Volume One* (San Francisco: HarperSanFrancisco, 1987), p. 67.
3. Stephen Charnock, *Discourses Upon the Existence and Attributes of God, vol. I* (Grand Rapids: Baker, 1979 [orig. 1853]), p. 402.
4. Russell P. Spittler, *God the Father* (Springfield, Mo.: Gospel Publishing House, 1976), pp. 85-90.
5. Charles Hartshorne, "Pantheism and Panentheism," in *The Encyclopedia of Religion*, (New York: Macmillan, 1987), vol. 11, p. 169.
6. Cited in Russell Chandler, *Understanding the New Age* (Grand Rapids: Zondervan, 1993), p. 28.
7. Brian Davies, *Thinking About God* (London: Geoffrey Chapman, 1985), p. 197.
8. Oden, *The Living God*, p. 68.

# God's Power

God is able to do more than man can understand.
*Thomas à Kempis*

## Overview

Christians have historically affirmed the biblical teaching that God is all-powerful. For example, both the Apostles' and Nicene Creeds begin, "I believe in God the Father *Almighty*." Discussions of God's omnipotence, as this doctrine is known, can become entangled in philosophical or theological thickets. However, as we focus on what Scripture reveals about the power of God, we are freed to appreciate the wonderful truth that our human weaknesses and limitations do not bind the unimaginably great power of God.

---

*Read: Psalm 68:28-35 and Mark 10:23-27*

### For Discussion

*1. What kinds of powers would you like to have? Why? What might it be like to be all-powerful?*

*2. What do these passages teach us about the power of God?*

# The Texts

## *Psalm 68:28-35*

Psalm 68 uses an array of images to convey the might and majesty of God. A theme that runs throughout the psalm is that of God's great acts of deliverance. In the psalm's closing verses (28-35), the psalmist prays that God will again show the power he has previously revealed in his deeds done on Israel's behalf.

### *Summon your power, O God; show us your strength (v. 28)*

The Hebrew word translated "power" here and in verse 34 is used almost exclusively in reference to God. The Old Testament routinely reveals that power and strength are essential attributes of God.

For example, after Abraham and Sarah dismiss the possibility that they will have a son, God responds, "Is anything too hard for the Lord?" (Gen. 18:14). From Psalm 115:3 we learn that God "does whatever pleases him." Elsewhere in the Psalms we read, "Once God has spoken; twice have I heard this: that power belongs to God" (Ps. 62:11, NRSV) and "I have seen you in the sanctuary and beheld your power and your glory" (Ps. 63:2).

In Psalm 68 the psalmist recognizes power and strength to be part of God's nature, and prays that God will show his strength against the enemies of his people. Moreover, the psalmist realizes that it is this all-powerful God who empowers his people.

### *the God of Israel gives power and strength to his people (v. 35)*

When God bestows his strength on a person, on his people, or on Zion, "not only is strength a quality given by God, he himself is that strength."[1] The strength and power of God not only provide God's people a sense of security, these facets of God's nature also offer us an opportunity for praise, as, for example, in Psalm 29:1,

"Ascribe to the LORD, O mighty ones, ascribe to the Lord glory and strength."

This closing verse summarizes the entire psalm. As James Luther Mays comments, "The confessional purpose of this psalm is to remember and represent the Lord as the power and strength of his people. ... The congregation confesses that it depends daily upon the victory of God for its salvation."[2]

And John Calvin observes that without our reliance on God's strength and power "it is impossible that we could stand one moment in the contest with such enemies as Satan, sin, and the world."

## Mark 10:23-27

Jesus' encounter with the rich young ruler comes toward the end of a passage in which he has been teaching about entering the Kingdom of God. That God alone has the power to save, and that he has the power to save any person from any situation, are specific illustrations of God's omnipotence.

### With man this is impossible (v. 27)

In summarizing the doctrine of salvation, Jesus utterly astonished his disciples (v. 26). Popular Jewish morality held that wealth was a sign of God's favor – the more money and property one possessed, the more certain that person had received God's favor and would therefore enter God's Kingdom. Jesus turned upside down the accepted Jewish standards of his day, teaching that if salvation depended on human efforts it would be impossible for everyone, even those whose material prosperity seemed a sure sign of God's favor.

Jesus explained that even those people commonly assumed to be the special objects of God's favor do not have the capacity to bring themselves into God's kingdom. God's power, however, is not subject to human limitations. The person who trusts in position or possessions is not saved (see Ps. 52:1-7). Only the saving power of God is sufficient to bring sinful human beings into right relationship with God. God has the power, and the will, to save those who cannot save themselves.

### all things are possible with God (v. 27)

The Greek words translated "possible" and "power" both come from *dunamai* (the root of "dynamite"), meaning "being able, having the capacity."

While the specific occasion of this discussion between Jesus and his disciples concerned human salvation, his assertion that "*all things* are possible [*dunata*] with God" infinitely extends the sphere of God's capacity and ability. Indeed, Jesus' declaration shows us that God's power stretches far beyond the limits of human imagination. As Paul writes to the Ephesians, "Now to him who is able to do immeasurably more than all we ask or imagine, according to his power [*dunameno*] ..." (Eph. 3:20).

As with several other historic Christian teachings, the doctrine of God's omnipotence is not explained in detail in the Bible. But placing together such passages as these helps us to see that Christians rightly worship God as Almighty, All-Powerful, Omnipotent.

### For Discussion

1. What are some common human understandings and uses of power?

2. What are some of the similarities between the ways people use their power and the ways God uses his power? What are some of the differences?

3. How does the Bible help us see and understand the power of God?

4. In what ways have you seen God's power displayed in your life?

# The Teachings

These passages help to illustrate the doctrine of God's omnipotence, and to distinguish this biblical understanding of God's power from such culturally popular notions as "The Force."

## *God is Omnipotent*

To say that God is "omnipotent" is to say that God has all power, that with God all things are possible.

God is called "the Almighty" in both the Old and New Testaments. In Lesson 6 we saw how God revealed himself to Abram as *el-shaddai*. The Greek equivalent to this term, *pantokrator*, appears 10 times in the New Testament, where it is usually translated "Almighty." Perhaps the most familiar alternate translation is found in Revelation 19:6, "And I heard as it were the voice of a great multitude, and as the voice of many waters, and as the voice of mighty thunderings, saying, Alleluia: for the Lord God *omnipotent* reigneth" (KJV).

God's power and God's reign go hand in hand. "To reign, God must have power, and to reign sovereignly, He must have all power."[3] As we seek to understand what Scripture teaches about God's unlimited power we learn that:

1. *Nothing is too hard for God to do*. Jeremiah prays, "Ah, Sovereign LORD, you have made the heavens and the earth by your great power and outstretched arm. Nothing is too hard for you" (Jer. 32:17). And God rhetorically responds, "I am the LORD, the God of all mankind. Is anything too hard for me?" (Jer. 32:27). This does not mean that God can do things that are by definition impossible, such as make a square circle. It does not diminish God's power to acknowledge that God cannot do that which by definition cannot be done. Rather, to say that nothing is too hard for God to do is to say that God has the ability and capacity to do whatever he wills to do.

2. *God wills to do that which is consistent with his nature, character, and purposes.* There are, however, many things God simply will not do (see Matt. 4:1-11). Among them, God will not lie (Titus 1:1-3); God will not be tempted by, nor tempt others to do, evil (James 1:13); and God will not deny himself (II Tim. 2:13). That God will not exercise his power in ways that are inconsistent with his nature, character, or purpose in no way diminishes the reality of God's omnipotence. "It is God's nature to be self-consistent, and thus to act in a way that is congruent with God's essential being and character. God's power is expressed in harmony with God's wisdom, justice, and love, not as if God's power were completely detachable from these attributes."[4]

3. *God is never exhausted by the exercise of his power.* Unlike his human creation, God does not need to replenish the energy he expends. As the prophets and the psalmists proclaim, God does not faint, grow weary, or need to sleep (Isa. 40:28-31; Ps. 121:1-8). The extent of God's creating, sustaining, and redeeming energy is endless. While the energy of the created universe is subject to entropy (that is, it inevitably decays into disorder) God's energy is untiring, inexhaustible, and inevitably results in the fulfillment of his purposes for his creation.

## *Our omnipotent God is not "The Force"*

"The Force" is an enduring contribution to modern culture made by the enormously popular *Star Wars* movie series. In this cinematic universe, The Force is an energy field that surrounds and permeates all matter. A person who is in touch with (which means in at least partial control of) The Force is thereby able to move matter and minds in ways that seem miraculous to the uninitiated.

Some New Age followers claim that crystal gemstones or pyramid-shaped structures are uniquely suited to collecting, focusing, and channeling this supposed universal energy field. For example, a 700-pound quartz crystal, installed in a shrine in Hawaii, is known as "Earthkeeper." One visitor was given the following description, "The worshiper receives the vibration field of this crystal and attunes to it. It is God pervading and being all souls, all universes in the rarefied psychic vibration it constantly radiates."[5] Ultimately, such views are rooted in pantheism (see Lesson 8), the belief that "God" (or The Force) is simply another name for the total content of the universe.

In contrast to impersonal pantheistic forces, God's power is never seen in Scripture as an all-pervasive energy source that can be manipulated through mental concentration or harnessed through the vibrations of crystals. Rather, Scripture reveals God's power in terms of God's personal interaction with his creation, especially with his people.

Although we cannot explore it in detail in this lesson, prayer is perhaps the best illustration of the difference between an impersonal force and our personal, all-powerful God. God teaches us to come to him in prayer with our requests. And while there is far more to prayer than simply telling God what we want or think we need, the prayer that Jesus taught his disciples to use as a model is largely a series of petitions. (See Matt. 6:9-13.) Prayer, which Teresa of Avila describes as "frequently conversing with Him Who loves us,"[6] is not an exercise in manipulating God's power for our benefit. However, the privilege of prayer is a constant reminder that the all powerful creator of the heavens and the earth desires that we ask him to supply all our needs.

In an age when too many Christians have too little knowledge of what the Bible teaches about God, it is important that Christians be able to distinguish an omnipotent, yet personal, God who lovingly takes the initiative in interacting with his creation from an inanimate Force that can be manipulated at will by anyone with sufficient expertise.

In summary, the historic Christian teaching of God's omnipotence holds that God has the power to do whatever he wills to do.

God's power is in perfect correspondence with his presence, knowledge, goodness, and love.

---

### For Discussion

1. How does the historic Christian understanding of an omnipotent God differ from such concepts as "The Force?" How can Christians help others, including our own children, understand this distinction?

2. What things will God not do? Why not? Why doesn't this diminish God's omnipotence?

3. What does our understanding of God's power add to our knowledge of God's character and conduct?

---

# The Life of the Church

God's unlimited power can utterly amaze us. It can jar our accustomed frames of reference and free us from our habitual states of mind. But more important than astounding us with exceptional displays, God's unlimited power can help us see, at times with painful clarity, our limiting human weaknesses. When we have exhausted our own power, when human strength completely fails us, we can especially appreciate our need for salvation by one infinitely more powerful than we are.

Certainly most of us have experienced the sense of weakness that comes from having pushed ourselves to the very limit of our physical, mental, emotional, and spiritual capacity. If we are alert to it, such fatigue can afford an opportunity to learn more about God and about the ways in which God can act in our lives. For when we have entirely depleted our own resources we are in a position to appreciate most fully Isaiah's hymn of praise to our omnipotent God,

"He gives strength to the weary and increases the power of the weak. Even youths grow tired and weary, and young men stumble and fall; but those who hope in the LORD will renew their strength. They will soar on wings like eagles; they will run and not grow weary, they will walk and not be faint" (Isa. 40:29-31).

Remember, it was not until Paul had prayed, on three occasions, that his "thorn in the flesh" be removed that he heard the comforting words, "My grace is sufficient for you, for my power is made perfect in weakness" (II Cor. 12:9).

Paul also reminds us that we need not be embarrassed by our weaknesses, or by our need for a Savior: "I am not ashamed of the gospel, because it is the power of God for the salvation of everyone who believes" (Rom. 1:16). For Paul the gospel "is really, in spite of all appearances, power, and not just one power over against others, but the supreme power, the almighty power of God Himself directed toward the salvation of men, God's almighty saving power."[7]

God is the Omnipotent, the Almighty. And for that attribute our most appropriate response is thanksgiving and praise. For only an all-powerful God can offer us the strength and salvation we so desperately need.

## For Discussion

1. Have you ever been in a situation where you felt completely helpless? Have you ever asked God to do something only he could do?

2. What area of your life most clearly shows your need for God's power?

3. What are some things you might expect an omnipotent God to do that God has not done? Why do you think God has not acted in those ways?

4. How does the assurance that God is all-powerful influence your Christian faith and daily life?

## *For reflection and response*

How might the fact that God never tires influence your prayers?

Pray and give God thanks for his unlimited power and for his willingness to use his power to help his people. You may want to pray Psalm 77, or to use that psalm as a model for your prayer.

# Additional Resources

*The Problem of Pain*, C.S. Lewis (New York: Macmillan, 1962).
Chapters 2 and 3 offer Lewis' characteristically insightful reflections on God's omnipotence and God's goodness.

*Prayer: Finding the Heart's True Home*, Richard J. Foster (San Francisco: HarperSanFrancisco, 1992).
An accessible overview of many types of Christian prayer, emphasizing how we come to know God more through our prayers.

# Endnotes

1. Carl Schulz, *"oz"* in *Theological Wordbook of the Old Testament*, (Chicago: Moody, 1980), vol. II, p. 660.
2. James Luther Mays, *Psalms* (Louisville: John Knox Press, 1994), pp. 228-229.
3. A.W. Tozer, *The Knowledge of the Holy* (New York: Harper & Row, 1961), p. 71.
4. Thomas C. Oden, *The Living God: Systematic Theology: Volume One* (San Francisco: HarperSanFrancisco, 1987), p. 78.
5. Russell Chandler, *Understanding the New Age* (Grand Rapids: Zondervan, 1993), p. 103.
6. Teresa of Avila, *A Life of Prayer* (Portland: Multnomah, 1983), p. 52.
7. C.E.B. Cranfield, *The Epistle to the Romans* (Edinburgh: T&T Clark, 1975), vol. I, p. 88.

# God's Knowledge

When applied to God, superlatives become diminutives.
*Paul Tillich*

## Overview

In very different ways, and from very different circumstances, both Samuel's mother Hannah and the apostle Paul give eloquent testimony to the all-encompassing knowledge of God, a doctrine known as God's omniscience. As with God's omnipresence and omnipotence, the historic Christian teaching that God knows all things can seem somewhat confusing. But as Hannah, Paul, and the whole of Scripture teach us, our God is an all-knowing God. And knowing about God's knowledge adds depth and conviction to our worship and service of God.

---

*Read:* **I Samuel 2:1-3 and Romans 11:33-36**

*For Discussion*

*1. Would you like to be all-knowing? What would be some advantages and drawbacks of being omniscient?*

*2. What can we learn from these passages about God's knowledge?*

# The Texts

## *I Samuel 2:1-3*

Hannah's prayer for a son had been answered by God (see I Samuel 1). Her subsequent prayer of praise, echoed in Mary's Magnificat (Luke 1:46-55), begins with an outpouring of joy, followed by an affirmation of God's incomparability. After celebrating God's power and holiness, Hannah rejoices in God's knowledge, which is so thorough that it silences God's critics.

### *There is no one holy like the LORD ... no Rock like our God (v. 2)*

The Hebrew word for "holy," *qodesh*, conveys "the essential nature of that which belongs to the sphere of the sacred, and which is thus distinct from the common or profane. ... Because of his holiness, God is above the weaknesses and imperfections of mortals."[1] God's perfect and unlimited knowledge, which stands in sharp contrast to the limited and fallible nature of human knowledge, is one aspect of God's holiness.

A frequent theme of the Old Testament is that God ultimately cannot be compared to any created thing. Here the word translated "Rock" might better be rendered "Mountain," for it connotes, and thereby ascribes to God, unparalleled stability, strength, and permanence (see Deut. 32:4, 15, 18, 30-31). God's knowledge, like God's other attributes, is similarly beyond meaningful comparison with human knowledge.

### *Do not keep talking so proudly ... for the LORD is a God who knows (v. 3)*

This first section of Hannah's prayer concludes with a warning against human beings speaking out with pride or arrogance, since God is "a God who sees and knows every single thing."[2] This warning "is grounded in Yahweh's omniscience, particularly his ability to see through deeds to their true character."[3] Similar warnings are found in Psalm 75:4-5 and Proverbs 21:2; 24:12.

The Hebrew word translated "knows" (the phrase could equally well be translated "a God of knowledge") comes from the root *yada*, which "expresses a multitude of shades of knowledge." When used of God, it describes the various aspects of God's knowledge of humankind, which begins before our birth (Jer. 1:5) and extends to knowing all our ways (Ps. 1:6; 37:18).[4] In the Greek translation of the Old Testament, *yada* was most frequently rendered *gnosis*, the word Paul uses in Romans 11:33 (see below).

Hannah praises God for fully knowing his human creations. Paul's doxology recognizes that we cannot begin to fathom the extent of God's knowledge.

## Romans 11:33-36

This hymn of praise concludes the section of Romans where Paul has been considering God's saving grace, specifically the mystery of divine election. It is "an eloquent expression of wonder and adoration before the mystery of God's ways, the majesty of his mercy and wisdom."[5]

### Oh, the depth of the riches of the wisdom and knowledge [gnosis] of God! (v. 33)

Here Paul poetically praises a truth that human beings can acknowledge but not fully comprehend the immeasurable breadth and depth of God's wisdom and knowledge. This is the only time in the New Testament where the word *gnosis* refers to God's own knowledge, perhaps a reflection of Paul's intimate familiarity with, and imminent use of, the Greek version of the Old Testament, which often uses this term to translate *yada* (see above). That God's omniscience is lauded in both the Old and New Testaments underscores the consistency of Scripture concerning this attribute.

*How unsearchable his judgments, and his paths beyond tracing out! (v. 33)*

Earlier in Romans Paul teaches that God's invisible qualities are clearly seen in creation, "For since the creation of the world God's invisible qualities – his eternal power and divine nature – have been clearly seen, being understood from what has been made, so that men are without excuse" (Rom. 1:20). Karl Barth comments, "What is searched out in the deep things of God is His unsearchability (I Cor. 1:10). To know God means to stand in awe of Him and to be still in the presence of Him that *dwelleth in light* unapproachable. And so we are brought back again and again before the hidden depth of His Riches ... before the hidden depth of His Wisdom, His Thoughts, His Judgments, His Way!"[6]

*Who has known the mind of the Lord? Or who has been his counselor? (v. 34)*

This verse, almost an exact quote of the Greek version of Isaiah 40:13, adds emphasis to the statements made in v. 33, as Paul again affirms the unlimited knowledge and absolute self-sufficiency of God. There is no one who can add anything to what God already knows, nor is any adviser capable of giving God a better perspective on any situation. No created being can fully know the mind of God, for the finite cannot contain the infinite. And as Job discovered (see especially Job 38-42), no human being dare presume to instruct the Creator of all that exists.

## For Discussion

1. Why is it significant that both the Old and New Testaments teach that God is all-knowing?

2. What is noteworthy in the responses of Hannah and Paul to the omniscience of God? What is your reaction to the biblical doctrine of God's omniscience?

3. How is omniscience consistent with God's other attributes?

# The Teachings

The key teaching to emerge from these passages is the unlimited, all-encompassing nature and extent of God's knowledge. This biblical teaching stands against all human attempts to limit God's knowledge.

## *God's Omniscience*

Like God's omnipresence and omnipotence, God's omniscience continues to be the subject of theological and philosophical debate. Not intending to construct a systematic doctrine of omniscience, Hannah and Paul, through prayer and praise, simply recognize and give thanks to God for the unimaginable extent of his knowledge.

While we can humbly acknowledge attributes of God that we cannot fully comprehend, one possible approach to grasping how God can know even that which has not yet occurred is offered by C.S. Lewis,

"Suppose God is outside and above the Time-line. In that case, what we call 'tomorrow' is visible to Him *in just the same way* as what we call 'today.' All the days are 'Now' for Him. He doesn't *remember* you doing things yesterday; He simply *sees* you doing them, because, though you've lost yesterday, He has not. He doesn't *foresee* you doing things tomorrow; He simply *sees* you doing them: because, though tomorrow is not yet there for you, it is for Him. You never supposed that your actions at this moment were any less free because God knows what you are doing. Well, He knows your tomorrow's actions in just the same way – because He is already in tomorrow and can simply watch you. In a sense, He doesn't know your action till you've done it: but then the moment at which you have done it is already 'Now' for Him."[7]

As Lewis recognizes, the God who created time is not constrained by its limitations. Existing apart from his creation in no way limits God's participation within the created dimensions of space and time. (Recall the discussions of creation and pantheism in Lessons 1 and 8.) Indeed the whole of Scripture testifies to God's interaction with his creation, the supreme example being God's incarnation in Jesus Christ.

Another approach to God's omniscience is offered by Thomas Oden, who writes, "How can we get our sluggish intellects in touch with the awesome conception that God knows all? The divine omniscience is best viewed as the infinite consciousness of God in relation to all possible objects of knowledge. God knows past, present and future. God knows external events and inward motivations. ... God looks to the ends of the earth, sees the whole of the heavens (Isa. 46; Job 28), knows the secrets of the heart (Ps. 44:21)."[8]

Even though our "sluggish intellects" may find the doctrine of God's omnipotence difficult to comprehend, our grateful hearts can join with Hannah and Paul in humbly praising God for his unlimited knowledge.

### *An attempt to limit God's knowledge*

Perhaps the most frequent objection to the biblical doctrine of God's omniscience is that God cannot know what has not yet occurred. Such objections are often voiced by proponents of "process theology," a fairly recent school of thought that "accents that the universe and man are in a process of evolution and that also claims that God himself is in a process of change and development through his involvement in the universe."[9]

One consequence of claiming that God changes, that he continues to learn and mature is that the historic Christian doctrine of God's omniscience must be drastically curtailed. From the perspective of process theology, "to say God is omniscient means that in every moment of the divine life God knows everything which is knowable at that time."[10] Since the God of process theology is not the transcendent Creator of the universe but merely a member (or "the soul") of the universe, this being is as timebound as human beings. The future is thus "unknowable" to the God of the process theologians, which forces them to redefine the term "omniscient" in order to apply it to God. Of course, this redefinition means that their "God" is very different from the God worshiped by Christians.

One example of such substitutions is found in the essay "Six Common Mistakes about God" by Charles Hartshorne, whom many view as the founder of process theology.

Although he does not document his statement, Hartshorne declares that the doctrine of God's omniscience "is largely an invention of Western thought of the Dark or Middle Ages." He concludes that "the arguments for growth in God's knowledge, as the creative process produces new realities are sound. Thus ... our existence from moment to moment 'enriches the divine life.' And this is the ultimate meaning of our existence."[11]

The breathtaking assertion that the "ultimate meaning" of every human life is merely to enrich the deity of process theology is a dramatic departure from the historic Christian understanding that humanity was made in the image of God chiefly "to glorify God, and fully to enjoy him forever."[12]

Such radical redefining of words and phrases is not limited to process theologians. The same technique is employed by others who, for whatever reasons, similarly prefer to substitute a god they have invented for the God who has revealed himself to us.

One reason modern Christians need to study such historic teachings as God's omniscience, omnipotence, and omnipresence is that a basic understanding of these doctrines provides us with a standard by which we can measure novel theories about God's nature and actions and thereby discern truth from error. We set aside valuable time and make the necessary effort to familiarize ourselves with what the Bible says about God "so that we may no longer be children, tossed to and fro and carried about with every wind of doctrine, by the cunning of men, by their craftiness in deceitful wiles" (Eph. 4:14, RSV).

---

### For Discussion

1. How can God know what has not happened?

2. If God does not know the future, how would we have to view the promises he has made to us?

3. What are some responses that can be offered to the process theologians' view of a limited God?

---

# The Life of the Church

In commenting on his own approach to God's omniscience, in which he speaks of God as "outside and above the Time-line," C.S. Lewis observes, "This idea has helped me a lot. If it doesn't help you, leave it alone. It is a 'Christian idea' in the sense that great and wise Christians have held it and there is nothing in it contrary to Christianity. But it is not in the Bible or any of the creeds. You can be a perfectly good Christian without accepting it, or indeed without thinking of the matter at all."[13]

The "omni-" attributes of God – omniscience, omnipotence, and omnipresence – certainly challenge our conceptual capacities. They lie beyond the limits of human experience and we are able to understand them in part only by imperfectly comparing them to our own finite presence, power, and knowledge.[14]

We should neither be surprised, nor discouraged, by such difficulties. God's people have always found it hard to understand God's being and activities. Israel's attempts to create a God they could easily and fully understand ran "from the time of Israel's creation as a people (Ex. 32:1-6) to the post-exilic time (Isa. 44:12-20; 45:18-22)." Jesus himself, God incarnate, experienced this as well, for "From the time he was a young man (Luke 2:41-52) to the mocking that greeted his crucifixion (Mark 15:29-32) people found him difficult if not impossible to comprehend."[15]

However, Christians should not abandon, or (perhaps worse) delegate to religious professionals, the study of God's person and work simply because such study is difficult. The consistent biblical testimony is that God is all-knowing. Both Hannah, with her simple yet profound faith, and Paul, with his extensive theological training, praised the omniscience of God. Even if we find the speculations of philosophers and theologians to be unhelpful, we can be instructed and encouraged by the testimony of Hannah and Paul.

## *For Discussion*

1. God knows all our failings, yet still loves us without measure. How, then does God's omniscience affect our daily thoughts and deeds?

2. Must there be things God cannot know? Why or why not?

3. Could God be God without being omniscient? Why or why not?

## *For reflection and response*

Is it really necessary for Christians to learn about the "omni-" attributes of God? How does even a limited understanding of these aspects of God's nature aid our Christian faith and life?

Pray and give God thanks for his knowledge of all things. You may want to pray Psalm 94:8-15, or to use these verses as a model for your prayer.

## Additional Resources

*Our Idea of God: An Introduction to Philosophical Theology*, Thomas V. Morris (Downers Grove: InterVarsity Press, 1991).
   Chapter 5, "God's Knowledge," offers an effective overview of the doctrine of omniscience, devoting considerable attention to God's knowledge of the future.

*Process Theology*, Ronald Nash, ed., (Grand Rapids: Baker, 1987).
A collection of 14 essays by evangelical theologians and philosophers offering a "comprehensive critical assessment of process theology."

# Endnotes

1. Thomas E. McComiskey, "*qodesh*" in *Theological Wordbook of the Old Testament* (Chicago: Moody, 1980), vol. II, pp. 787-788.
2. Keil and Delitzsch, *Biblical Commentary on the Book of Samuel* (Edinburgh: T&T Clark, 1866), p. 31.
3. Ralph W. Klein, *I Samuel* (Waco: Word, 1983), p. 16.
4. Jack P. Lewis, "*yada*" in *Theological Wordbook of the Old Testament* (Chicago: Moody, 1980), vol. I, p. 366.
5. C.E.B. Cranfield, *Romans* (Edinburgh: T&T Clark, 1986), vol. II, p. 589.
6. Karl Barth, *Romans* (London: Oxford University Press, 1968), pp. 422-423.
7. C.S. Lewis, *Beyond Personality: The Christian Idea of God* (New York: Macmillan, 1948), pp. 17-18.
8. Thomas C. Oden, *The Living God: Systematic Theology: Volume One* (San Francisco: HarperSanFrancisco, 1987), p. 70.
9. J.D. Douglas, et al., *The Concise Dictionary of the Christian Tradition* (Grand Rapids: Zondervan, 1987), p. 307.
10. John B. Cobb, Jr. and David Ray Griffith, *Process Theology: An Introductory Exposition* (Philadelphia: Westminster, 1976), p. 47. An accessible introduction to process theology by two of its leading proponents.
11. Charles Hartshorne, *Omnipotence and Other Theological Mistakes* (Albany: State University of New York, 1984), pp. 3, 26.
12. *The Westminster Catechism*, Q. 1.
13. Lewis, *Beyond Personality*, p. 18.
14. Thomas Oden offers this helpful summary: "God's way of being with the world is omnipresence. God's way of knowing the world is omniscience. God's way of influencing the world is omnipotence. In speaking of God's presence, knowledge, and power in creation, we are identifying *relational* divine attributes, those that emerge out of God's relation to the creation ..." (*The Living God*, p. 81).
15. Paul Achtemeier, *Romans* (Atlanta: John Knox Press, 1985), p. 190.

# Immanence and Transcendence

> In his transcendence beyond everything finite,
> God ... is not bound to any place 'up there' or 'out there'
> but can also be present within the world of finite realities.
> *Wolfhart Pannenberg*

## Overview

While God cannot be confined by space or time, it is equally true that God is always present with us. Paradoxical though it may seem from our human perspective, even though God exists apart from all creation, he works within creation, particularly in and through the lives of those who put their trust in him. As Moses and John show us, worship is our most appropriate response to the God who reveals himself to be both immanent and transcendent; to be always with us and yet always ruling over and throughout the universe.

---

### *Read: Exodus 3:1-12 and Revelation 4:1-11*

### *For Discussion*

*1. Do you find it easier to initiate a relationship with another person or to be approached by someone who wants to begin a relationship with you?*

*2. What can we learn from these passages about God's nature and about the ways in which our relationships with God begin and develop?*

# The Texts

## *Exodus 3:1-12*

Moses was born of Hebrew parents in Egypt and reared in the palace of the Pharaoh. He fled Egypt after killing an Egyptian who was beating a Hebrew laborer. One day, while tending the flock of his father-in-law, he saw a bush that was burning yet was not consumed by the flames. God's self-revelation to Moses through that burning bush leads to Moses' commission to lead the people of Israel out of slavery in Egypt.

*When the LORD saw that he had gone over to look, God called to him (v. 4)*

As most of us would do, Moses went to look at a bush that continued to burn without turning to ash. But once he did, what had begun as another just day became a life-changing personal encounter with God. Moses' old life of shepherding livestock ended. His new life as a leader of God's people had begun.

Notice, however, that it is God's activity, not Moses', that is the focus of these verses. Moses had not gone into the desert to meditate on how he might bring to an end the sufferings of his people. Rather, the burning bush was the means by which God, who knew every detail of Israel's distress, revealed himself to Moses, whom he had chosen to be the instrument of Israel's deliverance. When Moses turned to look at the blazing bush, he was not expecting to hear the voice of God. He simply wanted a closer look at this unusual sight. Not until God spoke did the revelatory significance of this event become apparent to him.

*the place where you are standing is holy ground (v. 5)*

The "flames of fire," here as elsewhere in the Bible, are visible manifestations of the holiness and the empowering presence of God. Recall that as the Israelites left Egypt for the Promised Land, "By day the LORD went ahead of them in a pillar of cloud to guide them on their way and by night in a pillar of fire to give them light, so that they could travel by day or night" (Ex. 13:21). And on Pentecost, those who were near the apostles "saw what seemed to be tongues of fire that separated and came to rest on each of them. All of them were filled with the Holy Spirit ..." (Acts 2:3-4). (See also the discussion of God's holiness in Lesson 10.)

### At this, Moses hid his face, because he was afraid to look at God (v. 6)

Moses' response to God's self-introduction is to hide his face. Only now has he become fully aware that he is standing in the presence of God. In this moment Moses learns that God is neither an abstract concept nor a remote entity indifferent to his human creation. God was near. Motivated by his faithfulness and compassion, God had come down to be with his chosen people. As Scripture shows, God often operates through human agents, and here Moses is called to be the one through whom God will free his people from their bondage as slaves in Egypt.

### So now, go. I am sending you to Pharaoh (v. 10)

Moses' call constituted a radical break from his past. Neither previously demonstrated faith nor any other personal endowment had the slightest part to play in preparing him to stand before Yahweh and be called to his vocation. These verses thus offer a classic description of the office of prophet as one that, while incorporating human personality, is initiated by God. Like the Old Testament prophets and New Testament apostles (from the Greek *apostello*, "to send"), Moses, who had been preserved by God for this moment, was called to be sent. As we saw in Lesson 3, God revealed his name as part of his commissioning of Moses to go and lead his people out of slavery in Egypt.

## Revelation 4:1-11

The Apostle John, Jesus' beloved disciple, author of the fourth gospel and three letters, had been exiled to the prison island of Patmos. As he worshiped there one Sunday, "I was in the Spirit, and heard behind me a loud voice like a trumpet" (Rev. 1:10). John then saw a vision of the risen Christ, who told him what to write to the seven churches of Asia Minor. Those letters are recorded in Revelation 2 and 3. Chapter 4 recounts John's second vision.

### After this I looked, and there before me was a door standing open in heaven (v. 1)

"John saw in heaven a door standing open, not that he might be able to look into heaven, but that he might pass in ecstatic state from earth to heaven, there to behold its wonders. ... This is the door of revelation."[1]

The Christian doctrine of revelation implies a God who must reveal himself if we are to know him, a God whose nature is so "wholly other" that unaided human hearts and minds cannot begin to comprehend his existence or his essence. These verses show us God's transcendence, and only as God opens a door in heaven are we able to glimpse his majestic might and his intimate concern for his creation. The call for John to "Come up," issued later in this verse, is reminiscent of God's call to Moses to ascend Mount Sinai (Ex. 19:24). It is an invitation to journey through the door that God has opened into his presence.

### At once I was in the Spirit, and there before me was a throne in heaven (v. 2)

This is prophetic language. It is not a reference to John's subjective feelings but to his objective experience as an inspired receiver of divine revelation, for "the hallmark of the true prophet was that he had stood before the Lord of Glory in the midst of this deliberative council of angels."[2]

*... jasper and carnelian. A rainbow, resembling an emerald ... (v. 3)*

It is the nature of gemstones such as jasper, carnelian, and emerald that the purity of their color results from their concentration of a single wavelength of light. The most pure and most brilliant gems are also the most rare. John's description of the one who was seated on the throne as a collected concentration of pure light calls to mind other biblical references to God as light (including Isa. 60:19; I John 1:5; Rev. 22:5). John's luminous description of God also recalls God's self-revelation to Moses at the burning bush.

*You are worthy, our Lord and God, to receive glory and honor and power (v. 11)*

Earthbound human beings take no part in this heavenly scene, where the theme is that of the omnipotent Creator reigning majestic. "[John's] visionary mind moved about in regions where *omnipotence* was recognized in a throne, where *omniscience* was indicated by innumerable eyes, where the very impulse to worship and pray found emblems in harps and bowls of incense."[3] (See also Lessons 8 and 10.)

## For Discussion

1. What are the similarities between God's self-revelation to Moses and his self-revelation to John? What are the differences?

2. What other biblical images of light come to mind as you read these passages? What do the characteristics of light, and the biblical references to God *as* light, teach us about God's nature?

3. Have you ever had an experience similar to Moses' or John's?

# The Teachings

While there are many parallels between these two passages, there is also at least one important difference: From a nearby bush God speaks personally to Moses, revealing his own name; from a distance John sees God sitting in awesome splendor on his heavenly throne and hears God's attributes praised by seraphim and elders. In theological terms, the difference between God's revelation to Moses and to John may be explained as the distinction between God's immanence and God's transcendence.

## *God's Immanence*

God's immanence (to be distinguished from imminence meaning "soon") means God's presence and activity within the world he has created, God's nearness to each of us. To say that God is immanent is to say that God is as near to us as our own thoughts, as close to us as our own feelings. It is to say that God himself is his gift to us, and that we are aware of God-with-us, Immanuel.

"Immanence" conveys the personal nature of God's interaction with creation, for the scriptures "continually speak of God's personal activity in the world. According to the scriptural metaphors and images, this activity is direct and immediate and continual. ... God is one who listens, who hears, who judges, who tests, who moves the hearts of human beings, who visits his anger upon people and who also shows mercy."[4]

The Bible also expresses God's immanence by saying that God dwells in his people: "For we are the temple of the living God. As God has said: 'I will live with them and walk among them, and I will be their God, and they will be my people'" (II Cor. 6:16); "And in him you too are being built together to become a dwelling in which God lives by his Spirit" (Eph. 2:22); and "No one has ever seen God; but if we love one another, God lives in us and his love is made complete in us" (1 John 4:12).

Our often dim awareness of God's dwelling in us, carefully nurtured and properly guided, leads us to desire God's "habitual presence." For while "most of the time the center of our attention is taken up by something else, God's Spirit is present at the edges of consciousness, enveloping us and everything else of which we are aware."[5] If we are willing to make the effort, we can become increasingly aware of serving as God's temple. As our awareness of God's immanence increases, every aspect of our lives – thoughts, words, and deeds – will increasingly illustrate the character and nature of the God who lives within us.

## *God's Transcendence*

In addition to being immanent, God is, equally and simultaneously, transcendent, that is, unimaginably above and beyond us. God is "wholly other." In his existence and his essence God is so distinct from his human creation that our limited senses are unable to perceive, let alone describe, his character and nature.

"The transcendence of God is frequently expressed biblically in terms of time and space. He exists before all creation (Ps. 90:2), and neither the earth nor the highest heavens can contain him (I Kings 8:27). [See Lesson 8.] ... In a manner that exceeds our finite understanding God exists in his own infinite realm as transcendent Lord over all creaturely time and space."[6]

God's transcendence certainly includes not being bound by space or time, which are simply facets of the created order. However, God's transcendence also means that God's attributes, e.g. knowledge, goodness, or holiness, are not simply superlative degrees of human qualities. Rather, our love is but a pale imitation of the limitless love of God; our knowledge is a dim reflection of God's all-embracing way of fully knowing all that is.

God's transcendence is denied by followers of process theology (see Lesson 10), pantheism, and Eastern religions. These alternatives to Christian faith either reduce God to the most powerful being within an eternally existing universe or they define God as the sum of all the members of the universe. The historic Christian doctrine of God's transcendence has even been attacked as "that orgy of self-alienation beloved of the fathers."[7]

Deprived of the biblical teaching of God's transcendence, Christian faith is denied. Individuals are left with only their own inner resources to strengthen and guide them. Only as we worship a God who is both immanent and transcendent do we possess "the full wealth of conviction" (Col. 2:2, NEB) that Christians ought to enjoy.

## For Discussion

1. How would you explain God's immanence to a non-Christian? To a Christian who was feeling far from God's presence?

2. How would you explain God's transcendence to a non-Christian? To a Christian who had perhaps reduced God to a "celestial best friend?"

# The Life of the Church

Because God is not limited by our categories of time and place, it is therefore possible for God to be present with his people at all times and in all places.

Whether through a bush burning in the desert or a door standing open in the heavens, the God who exists independently of creation makes himself personally known to those he has created. At the same time he makes known his desire for a relationship with each of us. Unlike ancient mythological deities, the God revealed to us in Scripture does not hide himself and then punish human beings for their failure to discover him. Nor is God a God who bludgeons his way into the lives of unwilling individuals. Rather, the God worshiped and served by Christians is a God who calls and invites, a God who encourages us to look and to listen for his presence.

Although in these passages of Scripture Moses experienced God's immanence while John experienced God's transcendence, both help us realize that the God-ordained response to God's self-revelation is worship. Through our worship we grow in our knowledge and love of the God who now dwells within us, as we live and move and have our being within him; who also reigns on the throne of heaven, now exercising his might and majesty in ways we cannot begin to comprehend.

## For Discussion

1. What are some practical implications of God's immanence for our daily faith and life?
2. What are some practical implications of God's transcendence for our daily faith and life?
3. Why is it not a contradiction to say that God is simultaneously immanent and transcendent?

## For reflection and response

How can our worship of God become an increasingly meaningful part of our daily faith and life?

Pray and give God thanks for always being near to us even though he transcends his creation. You may want to pray Isaiah 6:1-8 and Isaiah 43:1-7, or to use those verses as a model for your prayer.

## Additional Resources

*Basic Christian Doctrine*, John H. Leith (Louisville: Westminster/John Knox Press, 1993)

Chapter 4, "The Doctrine of God," employs several insightful analogies to explore God's simultaneous immanence and transcendence.

*Spiritual Theology: The Theology of Yesterday for Spiritual Help Today,*
Diogenes Allen (Boston: Cowley, 1997).

A much needed guide to the work of the "spiritual theologians,"
whose emphasis on cultivating God's habitual presence adds breadth
and depth to modern understandings of "spirituality."

## Endnotes

1. George Eldon Ladd, *A Commentary on the Revelation of John,* (Grand
   Rapids: Eerdmans, 1972), p. 70.
2. David Chilton, *Days of Vengeance* (Ft. Worth: Dominion Press, 1987),
   p. 148.
3. Martin Kiddle, *The Revelation of St. John,* (New York: Harper and
   Brothers, 1940), p. 68.
4. John Leith, *Basic Christian Doctrine,* (Louisville: Westminster/John
   Knox Press, 1993), p. 56.
5. Diogenes Allen, *Spiritual Theology: The Theology of Yesterday for Spiritual Help Today,* (Boston: Cowley, 1997), p. 2.
6. R.L. Saucy, "God, Doctrine of" in *Evangelical Dictionary of Theology,*
   (Grand Rapids: Baker, 1984), p. 461.
7. This statement was made by feminist theologian Rita Nakishima Brock
   at the widely reported ReImagining conference held in Minneapolis in
   1993. Susan Cyre, "PCUSA funds effort to re-create God," in *The
   Presbyterian Layman,* Vol. 27, No. 1 (January/February 1994), p. 4.

# Come and See ... Be Still and Know

What were we made for? To know God.
What aim should we set ourselves in life? To know God.

*J.I. Packer*

## Overview

In our final lesson, the psalmist reminds us that while we need to know such wonderful truths *about* God as his names and attributes, we also need to *know* God. Studying Scripture to learn about God from God's self-revelation is essential. The systematic study of nature and humanity, including such disciplines as science and philosophy, can also help us learn about God by reflecting on the things God has created. But in addition to intentional efforts to come and see what God has done, each of us needs to take the time to be still, to sit in silence, to feel God's love – to know God.

### Read: Psalm 46:8-11

### For Discussion

1. *What are some of the differences between knowing about a person and knowing a person?*

2. *What can we learn from this psalm about ways in which we come to a knowledge of God?*

# The Text

## Psalm 46:8-11

Psalm 46 is known to many as Luther's psalm. Christians around the world sing his paraphrase of this psalm as the hymn "A Mighty Fortress Is Our God." Its language and imagery, particularly in vv. 8-10, are eschatological, that is, concerned with the end times (see Lesson 2). The main theme of the psalm, which some have classified a "psalm of confidence," is God's presence with his people.

### Come and see the works of the LORD (v. 8)

The word translated "come" is a common Hebrew verb, found in a variety of settings throughout the Old Testament. However, the word "see," ("behold" in some translations) is found only 50 times, "almost exclusively in poetry or exalted prose ... [It] is apparently an exalted term."[1] This verb conveys more than mere sense perception. For example, it is used to indicate an immediate vision of God by people he has selected (Ex. 24:9-11), a revelatory vision granted by God to his prophets (Num. 24:4, 16), and spiritual understanding (Job 36:25; Ps. 63:2).

Paul reminds us that all people can know about God simply by observing creation, "For since the creation of the world God's invisible qualities – his eternal power and divine nature – have been clearly seen, being understood from what has been made, so that men are without excuse" (Rom. 1:20). God's acts in history are similarly available for study.

So while God has granted special revelations to some, God has made his works "visible" to all who will obey his command to come and see. Even those who are physically blind (as evidenced by those who approached Jesus asking to have their sight restored) are able to come to some understanding of the works of the Lord.

### *"Be still, and know that I am God (v. 10)*

The command "Be still" is derived from a Hebrew root that can also be translated "abandon, refrain, relax, go slack, let alone." Having taught in v. 8 that God's people are to be actively engaged in coming and seeing God's works, the psalmist here adds that we are to "know" God in those times when we abandon our self-directed efforts to comprehend him, in times when we deliberately refrain from intentional intellectual activity and simply allow our minds to relax into the presence of God.

The Hebrew verb "to know" can convey several shades of meaning. In the Old Testament it is used to express acquaintance with a person (Gen. 29:5), the sense of "to distinguish" (Gen. 3:5; Deut. 1:39; 7:15), and "the contemplative perception possessed by the wise man" (Prov. 1:4; Ecc. 1:18).[2]

All these aspects of "knowing" are well-suited to "being still." For while there is much to be learned *about* God by coming and seeing the Lord's works, there is a breadth and depth to our knowledge *of* God that only comes as we remain still, still enough to become acquainted with God, still enough to distinguish God from the false gods that would take his place, still enough to achieve a degree of "contemplative perception."

### *The LORD Almighty [Yahweh sabaoth] is with us; the God of Jacob is our fortress (v. 11)*

*Yahweh sabaoth*, "The LORD Almighty," may also be translated "The Lord of hosts." The former translation recalls God's omnipotence (see Lesson 9) while the latter reminds us of God's authority over innumerable heavenly beings. Whichever way the phrase is translated, the use of *Yahweh*, God's personal name (see Lesson 3) assures us that the God who has power over all creation, seen and unseen, is identical to the God of Israel. With this assurance, God's people may "relax."

"Because God controls both history and nature, the chaotic threat which both may offer to human existence may be faced fearlessly. ... Faith in God's protection, expressed so profoundly in this psalm, is both present and proleptic, reaching forward to the time of God's ultimate conquest of chaos and establishment of peace."[3]

### For Discussion

1. What are some of the ways in which we "come and see" God's works? What can we learn *about* God from our attempts to come and see?

2. What are some ways to "be still" and know that the Lord is God? How can we come to a deeper knowledge *of* God by simply sitting alone with him in silence?

3. What is conveyed in the psalmist's reference to God as "our fortress?"

# The Teachings

These verses identify two complimentary ways of "doing theology," that is, learning and teaching about God. The first approach affirms what we can and do know about God. The second recognizes that mere knowledge about God is insufficient – we need to know God.

### Come and see

Speaking thousands of years ago through the psalmist God said to his people, "Come and see the works of the LORD." An adventurous modern paraphrase might read,

"Take a look around you. Isn't my creation wonderful! Look as far out into the vastness of space as you're able. The more your technology improves, the better you'll be able to observe the glories of my handiwork. Then look inward at the marvelous complexity of the very building blocks out of which you yourselves are made; molecules and atoms, protons and electrons, leptons and quarks. Come and see the works of the Lord. For all that I have created declares my glory."

Historically, this active approach to learning about God has made positive statements about God's nature and activity. These descriptions of who God is and how God acts are based on what he has revealed about his character and conduct.

For example, when God reveals himself as *YHWH* (Lesson3), *el-shaddai* (Lesson 6), and "Father" (Lesson 7), we can learn about God's eternity, about his ability to provide for his creation, and about his love for his children. As we compile what we have learned from these and other self-revelations, we gain considerable knowledge about God's nature, abilities, and interaction with creation.

To be sure, even if we could comprehend all that God has revealed about himself in nature and the Bible, we would still be immeasurably far from knowing all there is to know about God. But as we learn more and more about the One in whose image we have been made, we learn more about his will to be in relationship with us, and more about the ways in which we are called to relate to one another.

## Be Still and Know

Coupled with God's command to come and see is his invitation "Be still, and know that I am God." This approach to knowing God may be characterized as seeking knowledge *of* God rather than knowledge *about* God.

The psalmist realized that neither ceaseless physical activity nor extravagant intellectual complexity leads directly to the knowledge that God is God. That reality was also recognized by the French mathematician/theologian Blaise Pascal, who spoke of "three orders" of human knowledge. According to Pascal, the order of the body, the order of the mind, and the order of the heart are completely separate, without any possibility of a gradual transition from one into the other.

For example, simply wishing for stronger muscles will not strengthen them. Muscles belong to the order of the body, not the order of the mind. The only way to strengthen muscles is to exercise the body. Similarly, certain aspects of God's created order can be apprehended and manipulated only by the mind, since such things as mathematical formulae belong to that order. [4]

Knowledge of God, however, comes only through faith and faith belongs to the order of the heart. Just as wishing cannot replace exercising as a way of toning muscles, so mathematical proofs cannot produce Christian faith, for logic and faith are also of different orders.

That is not to say that Christian faith is illogical or irrational. It is only to say that our knowledge of God does not ultimately depend on human logic and reason, on science or philosophy, for faith is of a different order. Abstract reasoning cannot produce a certain knowledge of God any more than lifting weights can yield the correct solution to a calculus equation.

## *For Discussion*

1. How would you explain the difference between coming and seeing God's works and being still and knowing God?

2. Are the positive and negative theological approaches to the knowledge of God contradictory or complementary? Is one way superior to the other? Why or why not?

3. Are you more experienced, or more comfortable, with coming and seeing or being still and knowing? How might you strengthen your abilities in the way that comes less easily to you?

# The Life of the Church

Christians have spent almost 2,000 years trying to describe the connections between coming and seeing God's creative works and being still and knowing the God who loves us, the God whom alone we worship and serve. One of the earliest efforts is still one of the best. Hilary of Poitiers, a fourth-century theologian from Gaul, wrote:

"Let us confess by our silence that words cannot describe [God]; let sense admit that it is foiled in the attempt to apprehend, and reason in the effort to define. I am well aware that no words are adequate to describe his attributes ... the best combination of words we can devise cannot indicate the reality and the greatness of God. The perfect knowledge of God is so to know him that we are sure we must not be ignorant of him, yet we cannot describe him. We must believe, must apprehend, must worship; and such acts of devotion must stand in lieu of definition."[5]

God can be known. God wants to be known. He seeks us so that we may find him. Indeed, "God so loved the world that he gave his one and only Son, that whoever believes in him shall not perish but have eternal life" (John 3:16).

The love of God has not been a separate topic in any lesson of this study because the love of God permeates all possible lessons about God. As J.I. Packer says, "'God is love' ... is not an abstract definition which stands alone, but a summing up, from the believer's standpoint, of what the whole revelation set forth in Scripture tells us about its Author."[6]

God's free creation of the universe is an act of God's love. God's self-disclosures – delivering his people from slavery, revealing himself by his name, providing for the needs of his people – are expressions of God's love. God's constant interaction with creation demonstrates his presence, power, and knowledge, and shows how deeply

God loves that which he has created. Our study of God is a faithful and loving response to the love of the God whom alone we worship and serve.

Our word "worship" comes from the Old English "worthship," which denotes the worthiness of a person to receive special honor. Worship "is something we do especially when we come into God's presence, when we are conscious of adoration of him in our hearts, and when we praise him with our voices and speak about him so others may hear."[7] It may be defined as "an act of attention to the living God who rules, speaks and reveals, creates and redeems, orders and blesses."[8]

The importance of worshipping and serving (the same Hebrew verb, *abad*, may be translated as both "worship" and "serve") God alone is a theme that runs throughout the Bible. When God called Moses to lead the people of Israel out of Egypt (see Lesson 11) it was "so that they may worship me in the desert" (Ex. 7:16). That God's people are to worship only him is stipulated in the second commandment, "You shall not make for yourself an idol ... You shall not bow down to them or worship them" (Ex. 20:4-5). And at the end of Revelation, when John attempted to worship an angel, the angel rebuked him, "Do not do it! ... Worship God!" (Rev 22:9).

The author of Psalm 46 knew that worship and service lead us to more knowledge about, and a deeper knowledge of, God. The invitation "come and see ... be still and know" does not exclude our participation in scientific and philosophical enterprises. Indeed, it assures us that the maker of heaven and earth wants us to know him through his creation. This invitation also reminds us our spirits are most readily attuned to hearing God's still small voice (I Kings 19:12) when we quiet our hearts and our minds.

The ancient words of the psalmist are startlingly contemporary as they speak to us today: "Come and see the works of the Lord . . . Be still and know that I am God."

## For Discussion

1. Why are the worship and service of God essential to our Christian faith and life?

2. What does Hilary of Poitiers mean when he asserts, "We must believe, must apprehend, must worship; and such acts of devotion must stand in lieu of definition?"

## For reflection and response

How is God's love for us expressed in the invitation "come and see ... be still and know"?

Pray and give God thanks for his love. You may want to pray Psalm 100, or to use that psalm as a model for your prayer.

## Additional Resources

*Christian Belief in a Postmodern World: The Full Wealth of Conviction*, Diogenes Allen (Louisville: Westminster /John Knox Press, 1989).

Allen shows how creation acts as a witness to God's existence, and that Christian beliefs find surprising support from contemporary science and philosophy.

*Knowing God*, J.I. Packer (Downers Grove: InterVarsity Press, 1973).

A classic collection of studies on God's nature and character by one of the twentieth century's most widely respected evangelical theologians.

*Worship, Community, and the Triune God of Grace*, James B. Torrance (Carlisle, U.K.: Paternoster Press, 1996)

Torrance stresses our need to recover a Trinitarian understanding of worship as "our participation through the Spirit in the Son's communion with the Father."

# Endnotes

1. Robert D. Culver, *"haza"* in *Theological Wordbook of the Old Testament* (Chicago: Moody, 1980), vol. I, p. 274.
2. Jack P. Lewis, *"yada"* in *Theological Wordbook of the Old Testament* (Chicago: Moody, 1980), vol. I, p. 366.
3. Peter C. Craigie, *Psalms 1-50* (Waco: Word, 1983), p. 345.
4. For an explanation of Pascal's orders see Diogenes Allen's *Three Outsiders: Pascal, Kierkegaard, Simone Weil* (Cambridge, Mass.: Cowley Publications, 1983).
5. Cited in Christopher Kaiser, *The Doctrine of God* (Wheaton: Crossway, 1982), p. 52.
6. J.I. Packer, *Knowing God* (Downers Grove: InterVarsity Press, 1973), p. 109.
7. Wayne Grudem, *Systematic Theology* (Grand Rapids: Zondervan, 1994), p. 1003.
8. Eugene Peterson, *Reversed Thunder: The Revelation of John and the Praying Imagination* (San Francisco: Harper and Row, 1988), p. 59.